by

Martha Gardener

Illustrations J. R. Harris

This book is dedicated to the men and women who have listened to my radio programs for over thirty years, readers of my magazine and newspaper columns, and my enthusiastic television supporters. Without their continued loyalty and help, this book would not have been possible.

Published by Wallace St. James Pte. Ltd.,
Singapore, London and Hong Kong
Australian Agent: Martha Gardener Distributors Pty. Ltd.

North & South American Agent:
ISBS, PO Box 1632, Beaverton, Oregon, 97075.

First Edition October 1982
Reprinted November 1982
Reprinted February 1983
Reprinted March 1983
Reprinted April 1983

Second Edition August 1984
Reprinted November 1984
Reprinted March 1985

Third Edition September 1985

ISBN 962 7120 01 4

Printed in Australia by Tripart Marketing Pty. Ltd., 51-57 Cubitt Street, Richmond, Victoria, 3121

about the author –

Martha Gardener has never pretended to be an expert but, like everybody's Mother, she is prepared to help. For more than thirty-five years on Australian radio and television and a weekly page in New Idea magazine, Martha continues to help men and women, young and old, with every type of day to day household problems. Stains, smells, cooking, washing and gardening; whatever the worry or disaster, people ring her talk-back programs or write to New Idea and 'ask Martha'.

Martha's mail contains requests for help from all over the world. Typical of the thousands of letters she receives each week, are quoted here:

"My kitchen has just been renovated with pale pink marble. It has stained where glasses have been put down. Can you help?'

J. Bobbio
Alessandra, Italy

"Thank you for telling me how to remove banana sap stains. I had six dresses confined to the darkest part of the wardrobe because of these stains. Now they are all wearable".

Angela Woodall
Townsville, Queensland

"Please keep your magazine column going. It has saved the situation for me many, many times. Good old-fashioned Common Sense".

B. Whiting
Beacon Light, North Queensland

Apart from a truly incredible memory, Martha Gardener's successful career can be attributed, in part, to her ability to live, learn and move with the times. With knowledge gained over many years, she takes the best of the old, mixes it with the best of the new, and shares it with as many people as possible.

In 1869 Mrs. Beeton said, "To be a good housewife does not necessarily imply the abandonment of proper pleasure or amusing recreation."

I present this book in the hope that it will lighten your tasks, allowing more time for pleasure and recreation.

Martha Gardener.

No matter how many, or how spacious the cupboards, no household ever has enough. Try not to overstock. You will anyway, it is an irresistible urge we all have, but don't overdo it, and make sure you always have the emergency cleaning essentials on hand.

BORAX – WHITE KING BLEACH – KIWI WOOLMIX
(or recipe on page 188) – SODA WATER – SALT –
KEROSENE – EUCALYPTUS – IMPERIAL LEATHER
TALCUM POWDER – CLOUDY AMMONIA –
NILODOR – MORNING FRESH DISHWASHING
LIQUID – BRASSO – LIQUID AND POWDER CARPET
STAIN REMOVER – NAPISAN – METHYLATED
SPIRITS (U.S.A. — SOLOX)

"Many people use Wool Mix for a lot more than wool."

"*I* get letters all the time from people telling me of practical new uses they've discovered for Wool Mix. I thought that I'd pass a few on to you.

For example, it's wonderful for your washable silk garments. Of course, unlike wool, you should rinse out your silks afterwards.

And Wool Mix is equally good for washable velvet items such as dressing gowns. It helps keep them really soft and cosy. Try it on your washable suede as well.

Naturally, anything made from sheepskin responds beautifully to Wool Mix, whether it be rugs, medical and baby care skins or even ugg boots! But to prevent hardening, you should sponge the skin side with brown vinegar before washing. Does your furniture have loose covers on the head rest or arms? You know how grubby these can become. If you use Wool Mix when you wash them, I know you'll be delighted with the results.

If you're a mother whose sons go camping a lot, you can get grass marks and all manner of outdoor stains off their sleeping bags by washing in Wool Mix.

You know, I sometimes wonder why it's called 'Wool Mix'. It really is so good for cleaning all manner of things!

COUNTRY HOMESTEAD
Eucalyptus
WOOL MIX

"I recommend this no-rinse wool mix for a lovely soft wash for woollens"

750ml

ACRIFLAVINE

Check the bottle to see if the Acriflavine has a water or alcohol base. For a Water Base, dampen the stain and cover it with Kemdex Tooth Powder, Leave for fifteen minutes, then wash in Napisan. For Acriflavine with an Alcohol Base, methylated spirits will generally remove the stain.

ADHESIVE
To remove

See ice-cream containers, also Blu Tack and Glue.

AFRICAN
VIOLETS

The time to divide and replant African Violets is the end of summer when the plants have finished flowering and are in a dormant period. Leave them for a few weeks to recover from the move before adding any feed.

ALABASTER

Rub soiled alabaster with a cloth dipped in turpentine, or, if badly stained, try powdered cuttle fish (available from pet shops).

Another method is to make a paste of chloride of lime (from hardware stores, some plant shops, or nurserymen) and water. Pack the paste on and leave for an hour before washing off.

Whichever method you use, polish afterwards with beeswax to give a good surface.

ALL PURPOSE
FLOUR

American terminology for plain flour.

ALLERGY Food allergies are very difficult as it is often hard to find recipes for those who are restricted to eating particular foods. Most large hospitals have a dietician on the staff who is usually able to supply dietary recipes.

ALLERGY See EGGS.

ALUMINIUM See Saucepans.

AMMONIA See CLOUDY AMMONIA.

ANGELICA

Angelica is a herb with many uses. The leaves can be used in salads. The stalks and stems can be crystallised for decorating cakes...

Chewing the stalks is an old fashioned remedy for flatulence...

ANGORA FLUFF Angora, Mohair or any fluffy woolly jumper or cardigan has a nasty habit of shedding. Half an hour in a plastic bag in the refrigerator before wearing, often helps to stop the hairs from shedding all over the place. Another system, is to spray the article with Scotchguard. It is better to try a little on the inside first to make sure that the Scotchguarding does not flatten or spoil the fluffy look of your garment. Another system is to lightly sponge the article with vinegar. That will sometimes help.

Mop us excess moisture quickly to prevent as much as possible from soaking into the carpet. Next sponge with white vinegar or soda water, then with cloudy ammonia. If traces of the stain still remain, a good dry cleaning fluid is often helpful.

Another method which has often proved successful is to mix a tablespoon of Kemdex False Tooth Powder in a small bowl of water and sponge the area with that, using a clean cloth. Always mop as you go, trying not to get the carpet too wet. A few drops of Nilodor will netruralise the smell.

One of the more successful methods of coping with any animal stains is to sponge the area with a fairly strong solution of Woolmix. If you don't have the Kiwi Woolmix available, make your own. The recipe is on page 188.

Remember, a hairdryer is very useful for drying the carpet if you have got it a little too wet.

ANISEED   See Fennel

ANTS

**ANTS –
in the garden**

I know that ants perform a useful function in the garden, but like everyone else I hate the little brutes and wish they would perform their useful functions somewhere else. Many of you will know the dismay of picking flowers for the diningroom table, only to find the table suddenly alive with ants. Vegetables too, can suffer an ant invasion. They are particularly fond of sweet corn and strawberries.

An old country recipe for keeping ants out of the garden is to mix 250 grams (½ lb) salt, with half-a-litre of water (1 pint), then mix in 5 kilos (10 lbs) of sawdust or bran and about 10 cups of molasses. It makes a very crumbly mixture to spread around plants and shrubs, and is not dangerous to children or to pets.

**ANTS –
in the house**

Someone once told me that Black Pepper placed under the rugs and carpets would deter both ants and silverfish. If you have a problem with ants, try sprinkling their tracks with Powdered Borax, Alum, or Talcum Powder, They hate walking over powder.

Another ant deterrent is to make a paste by boiling two cups of sugar with one cup of water and two tablespoons of borax. Boil for three minutes, put some on tin or plastic lids and place in the path of the ants. They are attracted by the sweet sticky contents and can seldom get past it. The containers are easily disposed of when the ants have gone.

ARGENTINE ANTS are easily distinguished from other varieties as they don't have the pungent smell when squashed. It is a good idea to check your local Council as some Councils provide an extermination service for Argentine Ants.

Any ants around the sink will be deterred by lemon juice. Just cut a lemon in half and rub it around the sink or in the general track of the ants. They hate lemon juice.

These are a good old-fashioned standby for the hungry children who keep running in and out with the cry "What have you got to eat, Mum?" **ANZAC BISCUITS**

Mix together 125 grams (4 ozs.) plain flour, 150 grams (6 ozs.) sugar, 1 cup dessicated cononut and 1 cup rolled oats. Melt 100 grams (3½ ozs.) butter and 1 tablespoon golden syrup. Dissolve half-a-teaspoon bicarb soda in 2 tablespoons boiling water and add to the butter and golden syrup. Make a well in the centre of the flour and stir in the liquid. Place in spoonfuls on greased trays and bake for 15 to 20 minutes at 120 degrees Centigrade.

A very effective natural spray for aphis is made by putting one tablespoon of Epsom Salts and one teaspoon of Condies crystals in a bucket of water and once every two weeks put a jam tin full around the plant. **APHIS**

ON ROSES, OTHER FLOWERS, SHRUBS, OR VEGE-TABLES. Seek the advice of a good nurseryman.

If a plague of aphis should turn your washing on the line from white to spotted black, never fear. Get a yellow plastic bucket, smear it with lanoline, hang it on the line and the aphis will turn from the washing to the bucket. Aphis are attracted to yellow. They stick to the lanolin, making it a simple matter to rinse them away.

Another way is to put the washing into a heavy green garbage bag, make it airtight and leave for several hours. The aphis suffocate and then it's easy to shake them out of the clothes.

Putting the washing in a tumble drier will also rid the clothing of the pests.

APPLES   Raw apples on clothing can leave a slight brown stain if not sponged off immediately with cold water on a damp cloth. Another method is to cover the stain with dry borax and leave ½ an hour. If possible, allow hot water to run through the borax.

Apples freeze well if placed in a brine solution of 1 teaspoon salt to one cup of water, for about ten minutes, then blanch in boiling unsalted water for about 1½ minutes. No sugar is needed but the addition of lemon juice or ascorbic acid powder is a MUST.

To prevent sliced apples from going brown, squeeze lemon juice over them. If you don't like the taste of lemon juice, the apple slices can be kept in cold water with a pinch of salt until ready to be cooked.

APRICOTS   Will leave a brown stain if left on clothing. Sponge off immediately and if the stain is still there, wash the garment in White King Powder. For woollen garments, use Woolmix.

Apricots freeze well but peel and remove the stones. Always use perfect, unbruised fruit for freezing. Stew or blanch.

Some plants, like some people, just don't get along well together Apricots do not like being near tomatoes. So remember when planting an apricot tree do not plant tomatoes near it.

SUGARLESS APRICOT JAM. Stone and cut the fruit, removing any bruises or blemishes. Cover the fruit with water and bring to the boil. Boil hard and reduce the fluid content, then add 1 teaspoon Gelatine for each cup of fruit. Without sugar, the gelatine is necessary for setting. This recipe will not have the keeping qualities of normal jam, so make it in small quantities, and keep in the refrigerator.

ARMS

Our grandmothers used a recipe for improving the look of their arms by mixing one part Spirits of Camphor and three parts Orangeflower Water. Massage this mixture into the arms working from the wrists to the elbows, then from the elbows towards the shoulders. Even if it doesn't improve the look of the arms, it is certainly a wonderful cooling refresher during the hotter months.

ASPARAGUS

This is a vegetable with a short seasonal life. Buy it when it is at its lowest price and freeze for out-of-season use. Use only young spears with tight tips. Discard the tough parts of the stalk, wash thoroughly and water blanch for two minutes. Do not use freezer bags for asparagus. Use a rigid container.

When cooking asparagus, use a teaspoon of sugar, not salt. This brings out the best in flavour, whilst salt has a tendency to toughen the delicate spears.

ASPHALT

Oil and grease tend to blend into the tar content of asphalt. With heat, the problem intensifies. It's worth trying Mineral Turps on this type of stain, spread over with sand and let the heat draw the oil up into the sand then sweep it away. Finish by scrubbing the asphalt with a yard broom and hot soapy water.

ASPIC

A jelly made from meat stock which has been sufficiently reduced by boiling to set firmly when cold. Gelatine may be added to the strained stock. Aspic should be served at room temperature.

AUBERGINE

More commonly known as eggplant, and is often served with meat dishes, sliced and lightly fried in breadcrumbs. They can also be stuffed and served as an entree or for a snack-type meal.

This vegetable freezes well either sliced or as a puree.

Avocado Stones

Sprout easily and can be an attractive indoor plant ---

Start by allowing the stone to dry. Then place it in a container of water. As it evaporates keep the water up to about $\frac{1}{3}$ from the base of the stone. Allow to sprout in water.

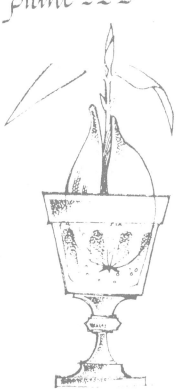

After sprouting transplant into a container filled with potting soil. Bury $\frac{2}{3}$ of the stone and water regularly --

14

To ripen avocados, wrap individually in dry newspaper and leave in a warm dry place. If they are sufficiently ripe, store in the vegetable section of the refrigerator.

The flesh discolours when peeled or sliced. The discolouration can be delayed by the addition of lemon juice. This fruit makes good ice-cream, although it is usually used as an entree, or with salad.

AVOCADO BUTTER. Mash one fair-sized avocado with a dessertspoon of butter or margarine. Add the juice of half-a-lemon, salt and pepper to taste, and a dash of cayenne pepper. Beat with an egg beater to a creamy butter consistency. Use on biscuits or in sandwiches. It is also very good heaped into a lettuce leaf and served with cold meat.

AVOCADO

Put a number of dried leaves under the griller and toast, turning frequently, until lightly browned, and crisp. Store in an airtight jar and crumble into casserole dishes to add a flavour 'with a difference'.

AVOCADO LEAVES Toasted

Beware of cement tubs when planting azaleas. If azaleas are to be planted in a cement container, the container must be treated beforehand. Put 125 grams (4 ozs) alum into the tub, then fill it with water and leave for three days. This neutralises the lime in the cement.

AZALEAS

Martha's Banana Special ~

Place the bananas in a flat dish for baking ~
Leave the skins on, but cut a 'v' shaped wedge
right along the banana ~

Remove the fruit from the cut out wedge and
place in a bowl with a little apricot jam, and if
desired a dash of brandy ~

Mix together with a fork then spoon the
mixture into the cut of the bananas in the
dish ~

Heap Pavlova mixture over each banana and
bake in a slow oven ~ Serve in their skins
with cream or ice cream ~

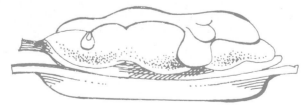

BABY CLOTHES DISCOLOURED

Even if they are well-washed before putting away, baby clothes which are not being used, can become yellow and develop brown spots. Soak the clothes overnight in a bucket of water with a handful of Napisan. Use cold water for soaking then wash the next day in fairly hot water. For woollens, use luke warm water and soak for one hour only.

BABY'S BOTTLE

If the bottom of the baby's bottle becomes stained, try putting in a teaspoon of Cream of Tartar, squeeze lemon juice into it and let it stand for half-an-hour before cleaning with a bottle brush.

BACON

A good way to keep bacon is to dampen a tea towel with vinegar and wrap it around the sliced bacon. If the bacon has been pre-packed, remove it from the plastic packet before wrapping in the cloth. Store in the refrigerator.

Change the cloth every few days. If you do not have cloth suitable for use, white paper towel is quite satisfactory.

There are varying opinions on whether or not to freeze bacon. It can be done, but is best in small amounts. Put dividers between each rasher.

BACON COOKING TIPS

Try dusting bacon rashers on both sides with a little plain flour before cooking. Remove the rind first, dust with the flour, and then fry. The bacon rashers will not curl, and the flour stops the fat from splattering.

BACON RIND

Rashers of bacon are less likely to curl during frying if the rind is removed before cooking. Save the rind. Tie it into bows and freeze. Use it for decoration and flavour on the top of casseroles.

BAKING POWDER Baking Powder is a combination of Sodium Bicarbonate and Cream of Tartar. Unless a recipe states otherwise, always sift Baking Powder with the dry ingredients before adding any liquid.

BAKING POWDER To test Because Baking Powder can become stale and lose its potency, it is always best to test before using it. Put a little into some cold water. If it fizzes well, the Baking Powder is fine to use. If not, discard it and open a new tin.

BALL-POINT PEN The inks used in ball point pens vary enormously. Most ball point pen marks can be removed from material if you act quickly, and dab the stain with Methylated Spirits.

If the stain has dried, use equal parts of Fuller's Earth (or talcum powder) and calcium chloride, mixed to a paste with methylated spirits. Leave it to dry, then brush off.

On vinyl couches or chairs, use hair spray. It sounds odd, but it does work. Just spray over the ball-point pen marks and wipe off. Then sponge with essence of lemon on a dampened cloth.

On synthetic materials, use essence of lemon.

Soaking the stain in milk sometimes works. After the soaking, wash in warm soapy water and rinse thoroughly. Repeat two or three times if necessary.

ON VELVET, wring out a cloth in fairly hot water. Then dip it in Methylated Spirits and gently wipe over the ball point pen marks.

See also INK STAINS.

Once peeled, bananas tend to brown very quickly. The browning does not affect the flavour but can detract from the appearance. This can be avoided by placing bananas, peeled or unpeeled, in cold water for about two hours prior to using.

Don't throw the skins away. Banana skins are good food for staghorn ferns. Just tuck them in at the back of the plant.

Bananas can be frozen either mushed with lemon juice, or straight into the freezer in their skins. Frozen bananas are only suitable for cakes or other recipes where pulp only is required.

BANANA

Banana sap stains, no matter how old, will be obliterated completely if you first dampen the stain with Kemdex False Tooth Powder. Let it stand for about an hour, then pour hot water over it. Any residual stain can be removed by soaking the garment overnight in Napisan, then washing in the normal manner. Steradent Toothpowder is also good, but be careful using it as it is coloured pink, and can be difficult to remove the pink from some white garments.

BANANA SAP STAINS

This aromatic herb is particularly good with tomatoes, or tomato-based dishes. Poultry and fish are often improved by the addition of basil.

A sprig of fresh basil in a bottle of white vinegar looks attractive and adds an extra zing to salads, fish and chicken. This makes an unusual and interesting gift. The artistically-inclined could make personalised labels for their friends.

BASIL

Basting is the moistening of meat before and during cooking. Spoon over or paint on with a basting brush. Specially prepared marinades, melted butter or dripping are suitable for basting.

BASTE

BATH   White or pastel coloured enamel baths can become discoloured, particularly if bore water is used. Fill the bath with water, add a large bottle of bleach and leave overnight.

Another method is to mix a paste of salt and vinegar, put some of the paste on to a soft cloth and rub over the bath's surface. A weekly application of kerosene on a soft cloth helps to prevent stains occurring.

BATH SALTS   1 kilogram (2 lbs.) Soda Crystals, 2 teaspoons essential Oil (Lavender etc.), 6 or 7 drops Sandalwood Oil (Sandalwood Oil does not perfume the salts, but holds the perfume which is added). The Soda Crystals are white, but can be coloured with food colouring. Food colouring is available from most health food stores and supermarkets. A variety of colours is available. To produce a pale gold colour, strong cold tea can be added, a few drops at a time, to the Soda Crystals.

One or two tablespoons of Bath Salts added to the bath water softens and perfumes. Packed in small jars and tied with a pretty ribbon, home-made Bath Salts make a great personal gift.

BATTERY ACID   Torch batteries can sometimes leak and stain clothing. The stain should be treated immediately with a mixture of washing soda and water, or bi-carbonate of soda and water. Mix to a paste, and for best results, leave on the stain until the paste is quite dry. Remove the paste and sponge over if necessary.

BAUXITE DUST   For those who live in the wide open spaces of Gove, in the Northern Territory of Australia, fine red bauxite dust poses a problem. So fine is the dust that it gets into everything. The only successful way I have found for removing the fine dust, is to soak the clothes in cold water to which Borax has been added. About two tablespoons of Powdered Borax to one litre of water is necessary. Soak overnight, then next day wash the clothes in hot water and Woolmix, but rinse in plenty of clear water.

BAY LEAVES

In dried form, bay leaves are readily available. An essential ingredient in bouquet garni, and a very good additive to many casseroles and stews. The Bay is an attractive garden tree, and can also be grown in a large tub for the balcony. For cooking, the leaves can be used fresh or dried.

BEANS

There are many varieties of beans, all of which freeze well and are easy to grow, even in small gardens. BROAD BEANS are podded, like peas before cooking but don't discard the pods. Use them for mulch in the garden.

DRIED BEANS can be a useful commodity to keep in the cupboard and you do not need to resort to the old-fashioned method of soaking them overnight before cooking. A much better way is to place them in a saucepan, cover with water, and bring to the boil. Boil for two minutes, remove from the heat, and allow to stand in the water for one hour. Then cook until tender.

BEANS – to grow. Beans are particularly good for the home gardener and can even be grown in a tub on a verandah or balcony. There are many different varieties and all produce a bountiful crop. Don't make the mistake of planting the seeds too early. Seeds won't germinate if the ground is too cold, but if you want an early crop, sow them indoors in peat moss then plant out when the weather is warmer.

In the springtime the seeds will only need to be planted about 2 centimetres below the surface, but as the hot sun penetrates the soil in summer, plant the seeds 3 centimetres down. Beans need plenty of water and fertilizer, and bear more if you keep picking when they are young and succulent.

BEDROOM FRESHENER

During the warmer weather, make bedrooms appear cool and fresh by cutting a small square of camphor into bits and putting the bits in a half-litre bottle. Almost fill the bottle with warm water, and when cool, add 50 mls. of Lavender Water. When the beds are made, sprinkle a little of the potion all over the room.

BEE STINGS Some people seem to attract bees more readily than others, and a sting from this insect is always painful. For immediate relief from a painful bee sting, gently remove the sting, and dab honey over the affected area. If you are one of the people to whom bees are attracted, it is a wise precaution to always keep a jar of honey at the ready.

Do make sure it is a bee and not a wasp which has caused the sting. For wasp stings, see WASPS.

BEER After the party is over, the sticky beer stains are often a worry. Sponge beer-stained clothes with warm water and Borax, using two tablespoons of Powdered Borax to one litre of warm water. Rinse in clear water before hanging out to dry.

BEER BATTER Sift 1 cup of Self-Raising Flour with a pinch of Salt. Make a well in the centre of the flour and add the beaten whites of two Eggs. Mix together with equal quantities of luke warm water and milk to make a runny batter. Then add 3 tablespoons Beer. Allow the mixture to stand for at least one hour before using. Beat it again before use.

BEER BREAD Bread is easy to make with beer instead of yeast. It may not keep quite as well, but fresh, hot bread never lasts long anyway. Mix together 1-¼ cups each White and Wholemeal Self-Raising Flour, 1 teaspoon Salt, 3 teaspoons White Sugar, and 1 tablespoon Wheatgerm. Mix in a 375 ml. (1-¾ cups) of Beer. Put into a well-greased loaf tin and bake at 190 degrees Centigrade for 35 or 40 minutes.

Spilled beetroot juice is something you should tackle immediately if at all possible. With kitchen paper, or an absorbent cloth, dab up as much of the liquid as possible. If the stain is on the carpet, cover it with Powdered Borax. The Borax will absorb the stain so don't be afraid to use plenty. Leave for a few hours then vacuum off.

BEETROOT

If the beetroot has stained table linen or clothes, soak in milk for a few hours, or , put the stained portion of the article in a shallow dish of cold water, with a slice of bread on the stain. The bread will absorb the colour. Always do this before washing the article.

Here is a way to keep beetroot which is very easy. Cook and slice the beet, take a cup of liquid in which the beet has been cooked, add one cup of vinegar, a few cloves and a bay leaf or two and keep in a jar in the refrigerator.

To clean and restore a bird bath it will be necessary to scrape off all the old paint first. Then thoroughly scrub the bird bath with one part bleach to three parts water. When the bath is completely clean, wash with a good detergent, leave it in the sun for at least a week to dry thoroughly. After that you should paint the interior with a chlorinated rubber-based swimming pool paint.

BIRD BATH

It's such a nuisance if a stray bird makes a deposit on washing that has only recently been hung on the line. If the bird dropping is dry, scrape off as much as possible and sponge with warm water and Borax.

BIRDS

On the car, or other paint work, get if off as quickly as possible with plenty of hot soapy water. Bird droppings can damage the paint.

NESTING birds can be a nuisance, particularly under the eaves of verandahs. To frighten the birds away from the nesting area, strips of cooking foil can be tied onto a string and put up so that the wind catches them and they tinkle together. The combination of glittering tinsel, plus the noise it makes, will often scare the birds away.

TO DETER BIRDS FROM FRUIT there is a product on the market called Scare-Away which is very helpful, particularly as it will not harm the birds. New products are continually being developed so check with your local plant seller from time to time.

Birthstones

Certain precious stones have always been sacred to specific months of the year. Ancient civilizations also attributed symbolical qualities to precious stones.

January   Garnet, signifying faithfulness.

February   Amethyst, peace-making.

March Bloodstone, courage and wisdom. Aquamarine was later attributed to this month.

April Sapphire, repentance and Diamond, innocence. In more recent times, only the Diamond is placed with April and the Sapphire attributed to September.

May Emerald, true love and Cornelian, contentment. The Cornelian is a clear red quartz.

June Originally Agate, for health and longevity, but latterly, Pearl or Moonstone is used for this month.

July Ruby, true friendship and Onyx, reciprocal love.

August Sardonyx, conjugal happiness. This is a type of quartz, banded with reddish brown and other colours.

September Originally Chrisolite, freedom from evil. The Sapphire is now the generally accepted stone for this month.

October Opal, signifies hope.

November Topaz, for friendship.

December Turquoise, for happiness in love.

See TEXTA, also INK and BALL POINT PENS.   **BIRO**

A good idea when baking biscuits, is to do so on a sheet of rice   **BISCUITS**
paper, obtainable from supermarkets. This saves the problem of
biscuits sticking to the tray. If the rice paper sticks to the biscuits,
don't worry, it is quite edible.

To keep biscuits nice and crisp, line the lid of the storage container with blotting paper.

Blanching is to immerse fruit or nuts in boiling water for two or   **BLANCH**
three minutes until thoroughly heated. This simplifies the re-
moval of skins from tomatoes, tamarilloes (tree tomatoes),
almonds, etc. It is generally considered best to blanch all
vegetables before freezing.

Never use too much bleach. One part bleach to four parts water   **BLEACH**
is usually sufficient for most fabrics.

If bleach is splashed onto fabric it will remove the colour. It is
sometimes possible to renew small spots of colour by matching
up with a waterproof felt pen. Just dab on a little of the colour
and cover-up job can be effected.

To combine gently two or more ingredients with a liquid until   **BLEND**
well mixed and smooth.

VETETIAN blinds are best cleaned with plenty of hot water and   **BLINDS**
any good detergent such as Morning fresh. It is better to take
them down for cleaning if this is possible, particularly if you can
get them out on the lawn, as it is possible to hose them down
afterwards. If they cannot be taken down for cleaning, make sure
you put down plenty of paper to catch any drips.

BONDED FABRIC is often used to make colourful kitchen
blinds. The kitchen usually has a build-up of grease and dust,
which collects on blinds and they are not easy to clean. Take the
blinds down, cover with a mixture of one cup of Powdered
Borax, half-a-cup of salt, and two tablespoons dry cleaning fluid.
Rub this mixture over the blind with the palm of your hand, then
brush down with a clean towel. That should get rid of quite a lot
of the grease. Then with a clean towel, wrung out until almost dry
in fairly hot water and Woolmix, sponge over any other spots. If
the blind is too badly stained, you could reverse it so that the
clean part is now at the bottom.

BLOOD
A fresh blood stain can be removed with a saline solution, made with a teaspoon of salt to half a litre of cold water. Soak or sponge the stain as quickly as possible.

If the stain has dried, pack it with a paste of Powdered Borax and a little water. Allow to dry and brush off.

BLOSSOM
To use Spring blossom in vases, it is best to cut the branches when the buds are just showing colour, crush the base of the stem before putting in water. When the petals begin to show, spray them with hairspray to stop them from dropping too soon. A little Cloudy Ammonia in the water helps blossom branches to last longer.

BLOW FLIES
In the early spring and summer, blow flies collect in porches, garages, or balconies and around doorways. Try growing basil in pots to put in these areas. It helps to keep them away. Another thing to do, is to crush garlic and leave on the ledges. Blow flies are not fond of garlic.

BLU TACK
Roll a little fresh Blu Tack between the palms of your hands then dab it over the old Blu Tack. A few dabs will remove it completely.

BOIL
Means to cook in liquid when the bubbles are bursting to the surface.

BONDED FABRIC
See CURTAINS, also BLINDS.

BORER
Kerosene or Cloudy Ammonia sprayed into borer holes generally kills them. Don't refill the holes with woodfiller until you are absolutely certain that all the borer has been killed.

Have your cupboards checked by a professional if you suspect borer.

Discolouration at the top of bottled fruit is often caused by the laquered lids becoming scratched. Get new lids, or cover fruit with cling plastic before sealing.

BOTTLING

See SHOES.

BOOTS

Used in casseroles, stews and soups to add flavour and aroma, bouquet garni is made by tying together a sprig of parsley, marjoram and thyme with a bay leaf. After cooking is complete, remove and discard the bouquet garni.

Stainless steel mesh immersers can be purchased for bouquet garni. This is most useful for the times when fresh herbs are unavailable and it is necessary to used dried herbs.

BOUQUET GARNI

Don't be put off cooking brains because you hate skinning them. Just put them into the freezer, leave until they are semi frozen, then skim off the skin with a potato peeler.

BRAINS

Is to brown meat on all sides in shallow, hot cooking oil, butter or fat, before adding liquid. Then cook slowly, with or without vegetables, in a covered vessel in the oven or on top of the stove.

BRAISE

For difficult to remove spots, try lemon juice mixed with pumice powder. Wash well with soapy water afterwards. Make sure the item is thoroughly dry, then polish with a good brass cleaner.

Lacquered brass sometimes develops spotting as the lacquer ages and begins to lift. If this ocurs it will be necessary to strip the lacquer completely. It is best to use the same brand of stripper as the lacquer. If you don't know the brand, seek advice at a good paint store.

Worcestershire Sauce is very good for cleaning brass.

BRASS

BREADCRUMBS Don't throw away left-over bread. Put slices in a slow oven to dry, then roll the hardened slices into crumbs. Store in an airtight jar.

BRICKS Smoke stains on bricks around fireplaces etc., can be removed by using a solution of water and White King. Use one part White King to 4 parts water, and scrub with a good firm brush, getting well into the bricks to remove the stain.

Use rubber gloves when doing this work.

Wash down if necessary, with warm water and a good detergent.

BROCCOLI Broccoli is a good vegetable for either pickling or freezing.

For freezing it is necessary to remove the coarse leaves and all thick woody stems. If there is any doubt about insects, leave the broccoli standing in salted water for about half-an-hour.

Do not attempt to freeze in large pieces.

Water blanch for three to four minutes.

BROIL Broil is to bake using dry heat, or by direct heat. In America, broil replaces the Australian term for grill.

BROOMS Clean brooms about once every month by washing in hot soapy water with disinfectant. If possible leave in the sun to dry. Always stand brooms with their heads upwards as it stops them from becoming twisted and pushed into shapes which makes sweeping very difficult.

BROOM HANDLE Don't throw away that old broom. Remove the head and drive a 7.5 cm. nail firmly into the end of the handle. Walk around the lawn pushing it into the grass. The holes will not be noticeable and will allow the water to penetrate instead of running off the top.

BREAD FLOWERS FOR JEWELLERY OR OTHER DECORATIVE WORK.

This used to be called Barbola work, but I have no idea how the name was derived.

Cut the crusts from sliced, very fresh, white bread and roll out thinly. Cut out petals to any shape you require and roll again. After the second rolling you may need to tidy the petal shapes. Now shape a flower by joining the petals together. A tiny drop of water is all that is necessary to get them to stick. On a very hot day, the petals may harden as you work, so keep a kettle on the boil and just use a little steam to keep the work pliable. Dry the flowers out by placing them in the sun, or in the oven, turned on low, with the oven door slightly ajar. When the formed flowers are dry, paint them with children's water colours, then spray with clear lacquer. Any good fast-drying glue can be used to attach brooch, earrings or necklace fittings to the flowers. Larger flowers can be made to decorate vases, jewellery boxes, etc.

BRONZE   A lot of cutlery, goblets, etc. are made in Thailand from bronze. They look wonderful at the time of purchase, but unfortunately the sheen doesn't seem to last very long. Try cleaning bronze with Worcestershire Sauce, then lightly rub over with cooking oil before putting away.

BRUISE   Bruise means to crush, to intensify the flavour. The term is usually used with herbs such as garlic or ginger.

BRUSSELS SPROUTS   Brussels sprouts freeze well but only select medium or small dark heads.

Soak as for broccoli to remove insects. Water blanch for about two minutes. The flavour of brussels sprouts can be enhanced by the addition of a little chopped bacon and a small sprinkling of powdered ginger.

After you have finished cooking, put a little butter into the brussels sprouts and toss them in the bacon and ginger.

BUBBLE GUM   Should you have the misfortune of sitting on a blob of bubble gum, or if you should have it adhered to any of your clothes, place the garment in the freezer until the gum is hard enough to chip off. Remove any remaining residue or colour by sponging with eucalyptus. If the carpet has bubble gum on it, pack the bubble gum with ice to make it hard, scrape off, then sponge over with eucalyptus.

BURNS   ON FURNITURE, burn marks from cigarettes and other hot things on a table can often be removed by rubbing with a little toothpaste. Always rub with the grain of the wood. If you rub some of the colour from the wood, rub over with a little matching shoe polish to bring the colour back.

ON COOKING UTENSILS, see SAUCEPANS.

See also FURNITURE.

Put a couple of slices of lemon into the cabbage when cooking it. **CABBAGE**
This will prevent the smell of cabbage from going all over the
house.

If butter cakes have a tendency to dry, or brown on the bottom, **CAKES**
they can be kept moist by putting a dish of water on the floor of
the oven.

For fruit cakes, two layers of brown paper are needed to line the
tin. A layer of salt between the two bottom layers saves the cake
from drying and burning. To prevent a fruit cake burning on top,
add a layer of brown paper half way through cooking.

See also WEDDING CAKE.

Camellias vary in the number of buds they produce, but they **CAMELLIAS**
should not be allowed to cluster together. Use your thumb to
remove some of those extra buds and the quality and size of the
blooms will be greatly enhanced.

To use camellias for table decoration, sprinkle a little salt in their
centres. It will stop them from browning if they get too close to
the candles.

If you are fortunate enough to have a camphor wood chest to **CAMPHOR**
store your furs and woollens and you find it has lost its pungent **WOOD**
smell, just rub the inside of the lid with fine sandpaper and the
smell will be renewed.

CANDIED PEEL The peel of citrus fruit could be classed as an aromatic condiment. The strong flavour comes from the essential oil contained in the peel, and is useful in many different dishes. When cooking, rather than waste the skin, why not make some candied peel. Chop the peel into thin strips, cover with cold water and slowly bring to boiling point. Drain off the water, add fresh water and repeat this three times. Weigh the peel and add an equal amount of sugar, and with just enough boiling water to cover. Simmer until the peel is tender and clear. Cool, drain from syrup, roll in strips and spread out to dry. If the strips are sticky after 24 hours, roll in sugar once more.

CANDLE WAX Dripless candles are not always true to their name. Don't risk them on your best cloth or table without first putting them in the fridge for twelve to twenty-four hours. For spilt wax, just cover with a block of ice, scrape off the excess and sponge with eucalyptus.

If heat from candle grease leaves white spot on the table, cigarette ash and water mixed to a paste will remove the marks. Brasso also works effectively, particularly on a highly polished surface.

CANDLEWICK BEDSPREAD To prevent fluffing, it is a good idea to Scotchguard a candlewick beadspread. Repeat the Scotchguarding process after each wash.

CANVAS Canvas blinds, chairs, and sails, get badly stained if put away soiled. Salt water is the best cleanser, so take them to the beach if you can, otherwise scrub them with salt and water. Trail the sails behind your boat, dry in the sun and sprinkle them with talcum powder – it will seal the sails for storing. Never use detergent on canvas.

CAPSICUMS

Commonly known as green or red peppers, capsicums are ideal for use in stews, casseroles, etc. They freeze well either whole or chopped. If using whole, use only very smoothly-skinned capsicums.

To freeze, peppers need to be blanched for about two minutes.

TO PICKLE CAPSICUMS, it is best to gather the pods with the stalks, before they are red. Put the capsicums into a jar. Boil sufficient vinegar to cover them. Allow a heaped teaspoon of salt and one tablespoon of Powdered Mace to each two litres of vinegar. Pour the hot vinegar over the pods. When cold, seal the jars tightly. The capsicums will be ready to use in about 5 or 6 weeks. Another method is to core, chop and freeze them.

CHOPPED CAPSICUMS. Separate fairly well after freezing, so you can use a small quantity for casseroles, etc., then re-seal and return the unused portions to the freezer.

CAR LABELS

Labels can be removed from car windows by soaking newspaper in Methylated Spirits then packing it over the label. Leave for 10 or 15 minutes and the label should almost slide off.

A cotton wool pad soaked in eucalyptus works the same way. Nail polish remover is also good.

CAR SICKNESS

The regular motion of a car can cause car sickness with children as well as older passengers. Keep a packet of junket tables in the car and if the children suck these it seems to settle the nausea. Allowing them to get out and run around for a little while also helps – it changes the motion. Some passengers perspire – try sitting on newspaper, that helps!

CAR WINDSCREEN

A film buildup often occurs on the inside of a car windscreen. Rub over with a freshy cut edge of a potato and buff dry with a soft cloth.

CARBON   Pencil carbon-paper stains on clothing can be removed with Methylated Spirits, but be careful not to saturate as it will spread. Put a clean cloth under the mark, and dab the stain rather than rub it. Be sure not to apply the Methylated Spirits directly onto the stain, put the spirits onto a cloth and apply the cloth to the stain.

Typing carbon paper is best removed in the same manner, but use Dettol instead of Methylated Spirits, then lightly sponge off.
(U.S.A. — use Solox or Rubbing Alcohol instead of Methylated Spirits)

CARNATIONS   These flowers last longer in a vase if you give them lemonade to drink. Don't let the children see you quenching the thirst of the carnations. They might start drinking from the vases.

CARPET   For carpet of wool, or mixture of wool and man-made fibre, use a foam shampoo or powder cleaner. Always spot clean before shampooing or using powder cleaner. Never get the carpet too wet. Always mop up any excess moisture and clean from the outside of the stain to the centre. To dry a carpet that has become a little overwet with cleaning, use your hairdryer. Never use a radiator, it can cause shrinking.
CARPET TILES, often used in kitchens, laundries, etc. can be scrubbed with Woolmix.

CAT'S and DOG'S URINE. This is another common occurrence on carpets. If the stain is a recent one, sponge with white vinegar or Cloudy Ammonia. Keep drying the carpet with a clean cloth so the stain will not spread. A few drops of Nilodor will get rid of any smell which may be left after cleaning. Also, see ANIMAL STAINS.

CIGARETTE BURN. If the burn is too deep into the carpet, there may be little you can do . Try going over the cigarette burn with dry steel wool, lightly rubbing it. If that doesn't work, rubbing with a weak bleach solution sometimes helps.

COFFEE. Treat as for tea.

DRY STAINS. If you do not notice a stain until it is dry, rub in some glycerine, leave overnight, and the next day sponge over lightly with a mixture made from 1 tablespoon of borax to 1-½ cups of warm water. Keep mopping up so as not to get the carpet too wet.

FOR FRUIT DRINKS. 1 tablespoon of Borax to 1-½ cups of water. Use a clean cloth wrung out in the mixture and wipe the carpet over with it. Try not to get the carpet too wet.

FURNITURE INDENTATIONS. Use a plastic spatula to scrabble around and get the carpet moving out of the indentation. Then hold a steam iron over the dented area. This should lift the pile of the carpet. This process may need to be repeated two or three times.

GREASE. Sprinkle the greasy area with talcum powder to absorb the oil from the stain. Cover the talcum powder with either brown paper or paper towels and hold a hot iron over the top of it. Do not press down hard on the paper. What you are trying to do is to draw the grease up into the powder with heat. Pressing down could only push it further into the carpet. You may need to repeat this process two or three times to get rid of any grease.

INK. The best way to tackle an ink stain on carpet is to cover the area with a handful of salt and leave it overnight covered with a dry towel to retain the humidity. This will allow the ink to be drawn up into the salt. If the stain is too old to respond to this method, use almost neat Cloudy Ammonia.

LIPSTICK. Sponge with Eucalyptus and then with Woolmix. You may need to repeat the Eucalyptus treatment two or three times to remove the lipstick.

NAIL POLISH. Dab the stain with a clean cloth and either Revlon or Faberge Nail Enamel Solvent. Do not use Nail Polish Remover as it may damage the colour of the carpet.

SOOT. These stains can be removed by covering the stain with plenty of salt. Leave it for about an hour, vacuum off and repeat if necessary.

TEA. The best way to deal with a spilt cup of tea is to sprinkle the area with plenty of Powdered Borax. Allow to dry, then pick the Borax up. It will be matted together by this time. Now vacuum.

CARPET STAINS

VASELINE. With kerosene on a clean cloth, dab rather than rub the stain. For any residual grease, sprinkle with talcum powder and leave for 24 hours. Finally, vacuum.

VOMIT ON CARPET. This often happens when there are small children about. As quickly as possible, wipe with a cloth and cold water, then Borax and warm water. Use 1 tablespoon to 600 mls of warm water. Don't get the carpet too wet, follow up with a sponging of Eucalyptus which will remove any odour from the carpet.

WINE STAINS. Soda water applied at once can be most effective. Keep mopping up with kitchen paper (preferably not coloured) or if left too long, use Borax. Dampen the stain slightly and apply Powdered Borax over the stained area. The Borax will act as blotting paper and absorb both the stain and the moisture. Leave until dry, then vacuum off. Eucalyptus will often remove a stale smell from the carpet.

CASHMERE

Cashmere is a very fine wool and should always be washed by hand. Use warm water and Woolmix. Always try to wash woollens on a fine day so they don't take too long to dry.

CAST IRON

Cooking utensils made from cast iron should always be tempered before use. To do this, wipe over with a little oil, sprinkle the inside with salt and allow to heat for about five minutes. Wipe well after this treatment and you will not be troubled with rust. Before putting the pots or pans away after use, always rub over with a little oil.

CATS

If you are troubled by a visitation of cats, you can keep them away from your favourite plants by sprinkling a little Kerosene or Cloudy Ammonia on a cloth and leaving it on the spot. For some reason cats don't like orange peel so leave it around with the cut edge facing upwards.

CAULIFLOWER

Cauliflower is a good vegetable for freezing and should be water blanched for 1 minute only. Cut up the cauliflower and use only small rosettes.

To prevent the smell of cauliflower permeating the house whilst cooking, place a slice of bread in with the water.

CEDAR

Cedar tables can sometimes develop a build-up of polish and finish up looking very smeary.

Put brown vinegar on a damp cloth to remove the smeary look, then polish with a clean, dry cloth.

CEMENT TUBS

Cement tubs are much used these days to add colour to smaller gardens, but it must be remembered that these tubs contain lime and to prepare the tubs for plants which may be allergic to lime, put in about 125 grams (4 ozs.) of alum and fill the tubs with water. Leave them for about 3 days. The tubs will then be ready for azaleas, or other plants that can't tolerate lime.

CEMENT PATHS   *See* CONCRETE.

CERAMIC TILES   *See* TILES.

CHANDELIERS   At one time cleaning a chandelier meant a day of agony, taking it down and washing every piece. Nowadays you can buy a spray which cleans the fitting on its hanging. The precaution, though, is to make sure you cover your polished wood furniture as the spray could mark it.

CHEESE   To keep cheese, wrap it in a cloth or put in a glass jar and keep it in the refrigerator. To keep the cut edge from hardening, rub with a little butter.

Another method of storing cheese is to keep it in a plastic container in the refrigerator, but with a couple of sugar lumps in with the cheese. This keeps the cheese mould-free.

Try using a potato peeler when slicing cheese for sandwiches. It is more economical and easier to slice.

To make an easy cheese sauce, grate 125 grams (4 ozs) of tasty cheese and mix with 2 tablespoons of plain flour, add this to 1 cup of heated milk and stir well, For cauliflower cheese, add a touch of cayenne pepper to this sauce.

CHEESE FRUIT'N NUT ROLL   A marvellous idea for lunch, pre or post dinner drinks, or just a healthy snack.

Beat until smooth, one packet Philadelphia Cream Cheese. Add 250 grams (8 ozs.) of finely chopped, Mixed Dried Fruits. Mix together well and then shape into a roll. Roll the cheese mixture in poppy seeds or crushed nuts. Wrap in foil and freeze for 10 to 15 minutes, then store in the refrigerator. The flavour can be improved by using fruit which has been soaked for 24 hours in 2 tablespoons of brandy.

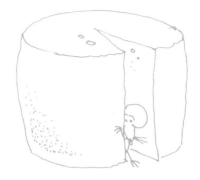

Sift together, 3 cups Plain Flour, 3 teaspoons Baking Powder, ½ teaspoon Salt, and ½ teaspoon Mustard.

Rub in 1 dessertspoon butter. Add 1½ cups grated cheese, and mix with 1 cup milk. This should make a moist dough. Bake in two small greased loaf tins for 30 to 40 minutes at 200 degrees centigrade.

CHEESE BREAD

Put 1 tablespoon milk in a saucepan with a nob of butter about the size of a walnut. Add 125 grams (4 ozs.) of finely grated tasty cheese. Stir over a slow heat until it bubbles, then add 1 well beaten egg. Stir altogether for about two minutes, then put into the oven to brown. Serve hot on buttered toast and garnish with parsley.

CHEESE RAREBIT

"An accident needn't be a disaster."

"Now even the worst carpet stains need be no more than an annoyance. All you need is in this box. A liquid for some stains. And a powder to use with the liquid for others.

As well as wine, they'll gently remove such horrors as golden syrup, soya sauce, margarine, suntan oil and beetroot! No single cleaner could ever match that. I guarantee it. Always keep Carpet Kit on hand. You never know when accidents will happen."

Martha Gardener

Martha Gardener

Martha Gardener's
Carpet stain remover Kit

"This two-part kit will remove most house carpet stains better than any single cleaner."

POWDER   LIQUID

250 g NET

200 ml
Martha Gardener's
Carpet stain remover Liquid

"Use this liquid to dissolve and lift the carpet stains listed on the back."

Martha Gardener's
Carpet stain remover Powder

powder with the liquid to dissolve the carpet stains listed on the back.

250 g NET

CHEWING GUM

Nothing will stop children from parking chewing gum where you perhaps may sit. If you do get gum on your clothes, put a block of ice on the gum, or put the garment in a plastic bag in the freezer for a while, then scrape off any excess and sponge with eucalyptus.

CHICKEN to crumb

Always lightly sprinkle chicken pieces with flour before dipping in the egg and breadcrumbs. By doing this, the crumbs won't part company from the meat when you cook it. Try adding some dessicated coconut to the breadcrdumbs. It adds a little extra delicate flavour to the chicken.

CHIVES

This is a very delicate herb used in many different cooked dishes as well as salads.

Chives grow well in a pot, but do not cut the leaves with scissors as this causes them to die back slightly, leaving an unattractive brown edge. Always pick the leaves with your fingers.

CHOCOLATE

TO MAKE CHOCOLATE, mix together 3 tablespoons cocoa, 1 cup icing sugar and 1 cup powdered skim milk. Add this mixture to 250 grams (8 ozs) of melted copha. Stir in a few drops of vanilla and allow to set.

For chocolate which has been dropped on the carpet, scrape up excess, then sponge with a tablespoon of Borax to a cup of warm water. On clothing, dry cleaning fluid is usually best.

CHOKO To serve as a vegetable, peel chokoes under running water, cut off the ends, halve and remove the seed. Simmer in salted water until tender and serve with a white sauce or melted butter.

Chokoes can be frozen. If small, they can be blanched whole, unpeeled, for 2 minutes. Larger chokoes should be peeled, cored and cut into quarters. Blanch in lemon juice and water; 4 cups of water to 2 tablespoons of lemon juice, for 3 minutes.

Choko bread, made the same as zucchini bread, is very good.

The sap from the choko vine can stain clothing. The stain can be removed by covering it with a paste made from Kemdex False Tooth Powder and water. Test a little of this on the garment first to make sure the colour will not be removed. If you are not sure about the fastness of the colour, make a paste with Borax and water. Leave it on for an hour. Brush off and sponge over with warm water and Woolmix.

CHRISTMAS See XMAS

CIGARETTES If you are a reformed smoker and can't bear the smell of stale cigarettes, leave a bucket of water in the room with a few slices of lemon it it. Another method is to burn candles in the room.

To remove the cigarette smoke stain from the ceiling of a car, sponge with a bleach solution. Use 1 part bleach to 4 parts water.

Cigarette burns on tables, providing they are not deeply burnt into the wood, can often be removed by rubbing with toothpaste. Always rub with the grain of the wood.

To peel citrus fruit quickly and easily, put it into hot water for five minutes and the peel will come away very easily.

CITRUS FRUIT

Any red wine looks frightening when it is spilt or splashed. You wonder if you will ever get rid of the stain. If it is spilt on the carpet, use kitchen paper to mop up any excess, and always dab, don't wipe. Then smother the stain completely with Powdered Borax. Leave it until the next day when it will be dry and the claret will have absorbed into the Borax Powder. It is a simple matter then to vacuum and there is never a trace of the stain. On clothing, use soda water, and always work from the outside to the middle so as not to spread the stain.

CLARET

Always keep a bottle of Cloudy Ammonia in the kitchen cupboard. It is used for many different cleaning jobs and is sometimes used in the wash water to soften fabrics.

CLOUDY AMMONIA

The best deterrent for cockroaches is to sprinkle their paths liberally with highly scented talcum powder or Powdered Sulphur. A commercial insect powder also helps. Cockroaches are most at home in dark, damp areas, so make sure that cupboards, skirting boards, etc. are all thoroughly dry at all times.

COCKROACHES

Sponge coffee stains with warm water and Borax. On washable fabric, if the coffee stain is old, dampen the stain, cover with dry Borax and let the hot tap run through it.

COFFEE

CONCRETE
Moss on

Moss on concrete can be dangerous as it is very slippery. To kill the moss use 30g (1 oz.) of sulphate of iron (available from hardware stores or nurserymen) to 4½ litres of water and scrub with a firm broom. Another method is to use crushed butchers salt. Rub it into the moss.

CONCRETE
PATHS
Oil on

If the concrete path is stained with oil, use one part detergent to six parts kerosene, leave this mixture on the concrete for five minutes and hose off. Phenyl (available in supermarkets) is also good. Use about half a bottle in half a bucket of water and then scrub with a hard yard broom.

See also kitty litter.

CONCRETE
Rust on

For rust on concrete use spirits of salt (obtainable from hardware or drug stores). Cover the rust with spirits of salts, then with sawdust and leave about 1 hour. Use gloves in case of a splash.

CONDY'S
CRYSTALS

A stain from Condy's Crystals should be treated with calomine lotion. Cover the stain with calomine lotion, let it dry, then brush off. If Condy's Crystals are spilt on the bath or handbasin, the stain can also be treated with calomine lotion.

CONTINENTAL
QUILT

See QUILT.

A hint from an old seaman has stood me in good stead when cleaning copper. Use Worcestershire Sauce on a soft cloth. Polish with a dry cloth. Another method is to use salt and lemon mixed to a paste, which is also very good.

COPPER

See VELVET

CORDED VELVET

Mop regularly with warm soapy water and add a little Methylated Spirits to the water. This helps the shine. If the floor shows any marks that are difficult to remove, rub gently with a little Brasso.

CORK FLOORS

If the surface has worn on the cork tiles, it is not a good idea to wet them. Just rub over with Turpentine on a clean cloth and lightly polish.

When cooking sweet corn don't add salt as this only toughens the kernels. A little sugar is all that is necessary.

CORN

The flavour of corn is best retained by leaving the husks completely around the corn, wrap in foil and place in the oven to cook for about 20 minutes. This method can also be used for barbecuing corn.

Corn on the cob, or as whole kernels, may be frozen by water blanching for approximately 6-10 minutes.

See LIQUID PAPER.

CORRECTION FLUID

For crisp crackling when baking pork, rub the rind with a little plain (all purpose) flour and seasoned salt prior to cooking. For the first 15 to 20 minutes of cooking, turn the temperature to high. After the meat is cooked, put it in the top of the oven and turn the thermostat back to a high temperature again for a few minutes.

CRACKLING

CRAYON If the children should use crayon to scribble over the wallpaper, and the wallpaper is washable, use toothpaste. Just rub it on gently until the crayon is removed and wipe it off. If the paper is not washable, try a little essence of lemon

MELTED CRAYONS on fabric seats are best treated by putting some ice-blocks in a plastic bag and covering the stain. When the crayon is hard, scrape the excess from the top. It is a good idea to use a plastic spatula to do this as it is less likely to damage the fabric. Next, cover the stain with talcum powder and over the talcum powder put a couple of layers of brown paper, then hold a warm iron just above the brown paper. Don't press down on it or you will push the stain into the fabric. When the grease from the crayon has come up into the talcum powder, spray the residual stain with Preen, and sponge off.

CRESS Generally regarded as a herb, cress is rich in iron, vitamins and trace elements. Cress leaves are often used in salads and are excellent for garnishing.

Cress was generally considered to be a good remedy for cleansing the blood and helping to relieve headaches.

CRICKET GLOVES Most cricket gloves can be cleaned by scrubbing with a solution of three parts water, two parts Methylated Spirits, and one part Cloudy Ammonia. Don't soak them in the solution, just put the glove on and scrub it with a nailbrush.

CRICKET TROUSERS The red stain from the cricket ball which gets on cricket trousers can be removed with a mixture made up of one part Cloudy Ammonia, two parts Methylated Spirits and three parts hot water. Sponge the stained area with this solution, then wash in the normal manner.

For KNITTED FABRIC test on an inside seam to be sure that the treatment will not yellow the fabric.

Gum Arabic water is good for stiffening crochet work. Gum Arabic Powder is available from any artists' supplies shop. To one litre of boiling water add 125 grams (4 ozs.) Gum Arabic Powder, Stir until the gum melts, then strain through a piece of muslin, bottle, cork and store for use later. For an average proportion, use one tablespoon Gum Arabic water to 1 cupful of water. This can vary according to the stiffness desired.

CROCHET
To stiffen

CROQUETTES

This is a mixture of raw or cooked meat and compatible ingredients, finely chopped and seasoned, combined with beaten egg or a very thick sauce, shaped, dipped in beaten egg, coated with breadcrumbs and deep fried.

When mixing croquettes, use Tomato Magic granules for added flavour.

CROUTONS

Generally used as a garnishing for soups, croutons are made by dicing, generally about 3-day-old bread, into small squares and sauteing each side in sizzling hot butter until delicately brown and crisp.

CRUMBED

It is most frustrating to go to a lot of trouble to cook crumbed meat, fish, etc., only to find that the crumbing parts company with the meat. This can be avoided by dipping the meat in flour before the egg and breadcrumbs. Using the egg and breadcrumbs twice gives a good crisp coating and is always tastier. Adding a few herbs and a little lemon juice is another trick which adds to the flavour.

CRYSTAL   For a good polish to crystal add a little Cloudy Ammonia to the washing water.

CRYSTAL DECANTER   See DECANTER.

CRYSTALISED FLOWERS   These are very good for table decoration, particularly when flowers are scarce in the garden. One method of crystalising flowers is to dip them into a thin Gum Arabic solution and then sprinkle with Epsom Salts. This is particularly good with holly leaves for Christmas decorations. The holly leaves look as though they are covered with frost. Flowers treated in this manner must not be eaten. For Gum Arabic solution, refer GUM ARABIC.

CUMQUAT MARMALADE   Wash and dry the fruit. Cut as much fruit as you like, thinly, and de-pip as you go. Cover the fruit with water and allow to stand for 24 hours. Next day, simmer the fruit and reduce. Then measure the fruit and add cup for cup of brown sugar. Boil until it gels. Bottle in hot sterilised jars. Allow to cool before sealing.

The Tomato Revolution!

Now you can add rich full-bodied tomato flavour to your favourite dishes with just the stir of a spoon!

Tomato Magic's natural. Contains no additives; no sugar or salt, no preservatives.

Tomato Magic's convenient. Use as much as required–a little or a lot– without fear of wastage, or problems of storage.

Tomato Magic's economical. Unlike tomato paste, there's no product deterioration; no mould; no waste. Doesn't require decanting for storage, refrigeration or freezing.

Seafood Creole with Tomato Magic | Hotpot of Beef with Tomato Magic | Cannelloni with Tomato Magic

All the taste without the waste

CUPBOARDS   Old cupboards can often develop a musty type of smell. When this occurs it is best to empty the cupboards and give them a thorough wash, preferably with a 1 in 4 solution of White King. Make sure the cupboards are thoroughly dry before putting anything back into them.

A few drops of Nilodor on a small pad of cottonwool will help to keep cupboards smelling fresh.

CUPS   Tea and coffee can stain cups. The stain is easily removed by rubbing the inside quite firmly, using your fingers, with either plain salt or a mixture of salt and lemon juice. If lemons are scarce, use salt and vinegar.

CURTAINS
Washing   Before cleaning your curtains always check what material they are made from. Many materials are dry-clean only. If this is the case, don't try to wash them, have them dry-cleaned. Light synthetics can be washed, but do so in lukewarm water, drip dry and hang before they are quite dry.

CURTAINS
Bonded   Bonded curtains can be washed with Woolmix. It is best to rinse the curtains after washing though. Some manufacturers recommend dry cleaning for their bonded fabrics.

CURRY CAKE

Beat	2 eggs, then add ½ cup sugar, ¾ cup oil.
Mix in	2 cups cooked, mashed carrots and the juice of 1 lemon.
Fold in	2 cups wholemeal flour, ½ teaspoon baking powder, 1 teaspoon salt, 2 tablespoons curry powder, 2 teaspoons ground ginger, 2 teaspoons dried spring onions, 1 teaspoon bi-carbonate soda, 1 cup natural yoghurt.

Place in a tin lined with greased paper. Cover with chopped nuts and a sprinkle of cayenne pepper. Bake in a moderate oven for 50 minutes. Serve as a savoury with drinks etc.

CURRY STAIN   Soak the curry stain in a half-a-litre cold water and 1 tablespoon Powdered Borax. If the stain persists, sprinkle dry Borax on the damp stain and allow cold water to run through it.

CUSTARD   Should your custard curdle while cooking, take off the heat, remove from the saucepan and add a little cold water and whisk firmly.

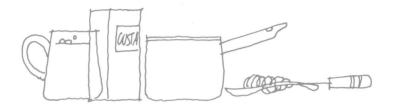

CUTTING BOARD
To clean   Wooden cutting boards have a tendency to absorb food flavours. These boards can be freshened up by saturating a kitchen sponge with cold water and a little bleach. Rub it over the surface for a minute or so and then run the cold water over it to rid it of the bleach smell. Let it dry thoroughly before re-using. White plastic cutting boards can be cleaned with toothpaste.

MOST IMPORTANT. Always wash thoroughly after cutting raw meat.

CYCLAMEN
To re-pot   Cyclamen should be re-potted at the end of summer. Don't bury the corm. I always think it's best to leave about two-thirds of the corm showing. Cyclamen can do well outdoors, although they do prefer a sheltered position. Cyclamen like the same soil conditions as Azaleas, so they can be placed near each other. Cyclamen flower best if they are fed pure rain water.

DAMP SMELL

After heavy rain, some rooms in a house can develop a slightly damp smell. As soon as possible, open the windows to let the air through, a heater in the room for an hour is not a bad idea. A few blocks of camphor placed in the room or a few sliced lemons in a bucket of water will get rid of the smell.

DAMPER

A good old-fashioned recipe for damper to be cooked in the coals is as follows. Mix together 2 cups Self-Raising Flour, ½ teaspoon Salt, enough water or milk to make a fairly stiff dough. This dough is usually then rolled around a stick and cooked over the hot coals.

DECANTER

Quite often, the stopper on a decanter will hold firmly and refuse to budge. To loosen and remove the stopper easily, pour a little glycerine around the stopper, stand the decanter in warm water and wrap a cold cloth around the top. Repeat if necessary.

To clean a decanter, keep your eggshells, crush them, mix with a little vinegar and add to the decanter, then shake well.

Uncooked rice with a few tea-leaves is also quite effective for cleaning a decanter.

To remove the stain of red wine from a glass or crystal decanter, put a tablespoon of Baking Powder and a cup of luke warm water into the decanter. Shake well, empty, then add warm water with a few drops of detergent and 1 tablespoon of Cloudy Ammonia. Rinse well before using.

DENIM Denim clothes are part of a daily uniform for both children and adults now. The material is good, tough-wearing and also very tough to iron. Try putting it in the refrigerator for a few hours. This helps remove the creases. Another method is to soak over-night with a small packet of Epsom Salts. Add a couple of table-spoons of vinegar to hold the colour.

DEVIL Devil is a hot seasoning added to a baste, marinade or sauce. Chilli powder, cayenne pepper, a large quantity of dry mustard, red pepper or Tabasco sauce are excellent for this purpose.

DICE This is to cut into very small cubes, usually about a quarter of an inch square.

DILL The seed of the dill herb was generally considered to aid in the digestion of cabbage, coleslaw, sauerkraut, cucumber, onions etc. The finely chopped leaves go with almost any food and the flavour is quite pleasant. Dill is frequently used in pickles.

Mix together 500 grams (1 lb.) wholemeal flour and 200 grams (6 ozs) minced meat, 1 dessertspoon salt. Add enough cold water to mix to a stiff dough. Roll out and place on an oven slide. Mark into squares and prick with a fork. Bake in a slow oven until brown. If your dog is only a pup, add 1 tablespoon Cod Liver Oil as it is good for building bones.

DOG BISCUITS

To keep dogs away from the garden, soak some old cloths in Cloudy Ammonia and leave them lying around in the most frequently visited spots. It will be necessary to keep re-dousing the cloths. About once a week would probably be enough.

DOG DETERRENT

On the carpet, sponge the stain with white vinegar, then wash the area with Woolmix. Do not get the carpet too wet and dry as you go with a rough towel, then finish off with a hair dryer. Sprinkle a few drops of Nilodor around the room to eliminate any lingering smell.

DOG URINE

It is sometimes difficult to know whether a doll is washable or not. If you are not sure, play safe and use a powder carpet cleaner or, from the chemist, a block of Magnesia.

DOLLS

See QUILTS

DOONA

See RATTLING.

DOORS RATTLING

See BLU TACK

DOUBLE SIDED TAPE

A twist of lemon peel added to a jar of dried fruit not only keeps out weevils, but also helps to keep the fruit fresh and plump.

Sixty seconds on "High" in the microwave oven brings dried fruit up to a soft, plump condition.

DRIED FRUIT

DRIPPING   To clarify dripping, put water in the bottom of a saucepan, pour in the fat and bring to the boil. Take off the heat and let the dripping set. When it has solidified, the water can be tipped away and the bottom of the dripping scraped to remove the sediment.

DUCK EGGS   When cooking with duck eggs, it is always good to remember that two duck eggs are equal to three hen eggs.

DUCK FEATHERS   Ducks are not easy to pluck because the pin feathers are difficult to remove. The best way is to heat some wax, spread it over the pin feathers and leave to cool. Pull off the wax when it is cool and the pin feathers will come away.

DYE   On garments that have picked up dye from other garments in the wash, spray the stained area with Nifty, leave for about two hours then wash in the normal way.

On LAMINEX, toothpaste mixed with Methylated Spirits will usually remove it.

EARWIGS

If you cannot see what is eating the leaves of your plants, it could be earwigs. They come out at night and an easy way to get rid of them is to use folded newspaper or a cardboard box in the garden. Put it in the garden at night and burn it in the morning. The earwigs go into the paper and will be burnt too.

Another method is to put 10 inch pieces of garden hose in places where earwigs gather. They will go into the hose and can be knocked out into the incinerator.

EGGS ALLERGY

Egg allergy is a fairly common problem and as many recipes use eggs for a binding agent it is necessary to have a substitute. Rice is the best substitute for many recipes, such as rissoles, which call for an egg to bind the meat. For meat-loaf, half mince steak and half sausage meat is a good method to bind meat without using eggs.

Grated carrot is also a very good substitute for eggs in boiled puddings.

EGGS Cracked

To remove a cracked egg which has stuck to the carton, dampen the carton and gently pull away. Should you lose a little of the white, a tablespoon of water will make up the moisture content.

EGGS Cracking   Eggs will often crack whilst being boiled. To prevent this, pierce with a darning needle or hold under a cold tap before plunging into hot water. A little vinegar, or salt, in the water also helps.

EGGS Keeping   The yolk of eggs can be kept quite well if placed in a jar with a little water on the top, and cover with plastic food wrap. Keep in the refrigerator.

Egg-whites freeze well, but leave the number clearly marked on the container, in case you forget.

Pickled eggs are excellent eaten with cold meat etc. The eggs should be boiled hard and then shelled. When quite cold pour over sufficient vinegar to cover them. The vinegar should have been previously boiled with the usual spices for pickling. Secure the jars tightly and keep until the eggs begin to change colour. **EGGS PICKLED**

Eggs will keep fresh for at least 3 months if rubbed with Vaseline. Refrigeration is not necesary, but keep in a cool place. **EGGS Preserving**

To make scrambled eggs go further, add a tablespoon of evaporated milk for every two eggs. Do not beat the egg whites in a plastic bowl, the bowl may retain a little grease and this prevents the eggs from whipping firmly. **EGGS Scrambled**

Don't depend on your nose to know if an egg is fresh, try an easier way. Put the egg into a container of water. If it sinks to the bottom, it is fresh. On the other hand, if it floats to the top, it is certainly not fresh and should be thrown away. **EGGS To test**

A tiny pinch of cream of tartar added to egg whites before beating makes them froth more quickly and the whites will be stiffer when beaten. Egg whites will not beat well if very fresh, or if taken straight from the refrigerator. Room temperature is best. **EGG WHITES**

EGGPLANT *See* AUBERGINE

ELECTRIC JUG
or KETTLE
Electric jugs or kettles often become discoloured. To remove the discolouration, fill the jug with water, add half-a-cup of vinegar, bring it to the boil and continue to boil for a few minutes. You may need to do this a couple of times to remove all the marks.

ENAMEL
Enamel scratches very easily, so to clean it, use Bon Ami fine powder cleanser. Toothpaste is also very good.

If a white enamel bath has become discoloured, use a good bleach such as White King. Fill the bath and add 1 full bottle of bleach. Leave overnight if possible.

If white enamel cooking utensils have become discoloured, stand them in warm water and Borax. About four tablespoons of Borax to four cups of water. This will restore the enamelware to white again.

EUCALYPTUS
For stains of unknown origin, or stains which have dried, a dab of eucalyptus is often a good idea. Eucalyptus is also good for removing many glue stains.

See PEACOCK FEATHERS **FEATHERS**

This is a very good fruit, ideal as a sweet or salad item. Once peeled all the fruit including the seeds, can be eaten. Feijoas are ideal for jam, jelly and for chutney. Peel under water to avoid sticky hands. **FEIJOA**

Simmer 500 grams (1 lb.) Mixed Dried Fruit in enough water to almost cover the fruit for 15 minutes. Allow to cool. Remove the stones from the prunes. Chop the rest of the fruit roughly. Top and tail 1-½ kilos (3 lbs.) of feijoas. Slice finely. Do not peel. Add the feijoas to the fruit mixture. Then add 125 grams (4 ozs.) Glace Ginger, 1 tablespoon salt, 4 small cloves Garlic, finely chopped, 1 teaspoon Cayenne Papper, 1 tablespoon Tomato Magic (or tomato paste) and 500 grams (1 lb.) Raw Sugar. Add just enough brown vinegar to cover the mixture. Boil for approximately 1 hour. Bottle and seal while hot. **FEIJOA CHUTNEY**

Cut 1 kilo (2 lbs.) feijoas roughly. do not peel the fruit. Cover fruit with cold water. Boil and simmer gently for about 20 minutes, or until the fruit is soft. Strain off the liquid through a fine sieve or muslin bag. Measure the liquid. Add a cup of sugar for every cup of liquid. Boil and allow to simmer fairly fast for about 20 minutes, or until the jelly sets when tested. **FEIJOA JELLY**

FELT PEN MARKS

On synthetic fabrics, equal parts of Calcium Chloride and Fuller's Earth mixed to a paste with a little Methylated Spirits sometimes works. Cover the stain and leave until the paste is dry, then brush off and wash in the normal way.

On VINYL, care will need to be taken not to remove the colour from the vinyl. **It is always a good idea to try a little of whatever you are using on the underneath part of the vinyl where it won't show.** First try Methylated Spirits, but as some felt pens are waterproof a different solvent may be required. Mineral Turpentine, nail polish remover, or hairspray can be effective.

FENNEL

This herb has a very light aniseed-type flavour and is ideal with fish, salad and spaghetti sauces.

FERNS

Potted ferns are most attractive indoor plants, and are also an effective deterrent to flies. Place a hanging basket, or a pot containing ferns near the door or a window where the flies come in. It may not stop a really determined fly, but the timid ones will go elsewhere.

FIGS
To dry

Figs can be dried in a cool oven, or out in the sun. It is best to dry figs whole, leaving a tiny bit of stalk on the fruit. First blanch the figs by immersing them in boiling water for about four minutes. Then plunge into cold water immediately for about 30 seconds. Remove the surface moisture by shaking them in a dry towel, then spread the fruit on trays for drying. The oven temperature should be no more than 115 degrees Fahr., and leave for about 2 hours. The oven heat can now be increased to about 145 degrees Fahr., and the oven door should be kept open all the time, allowing the damp air to escape. When thoroughly dry, remove from the oven and leave overnight. If there is any sign of dampness next day, return them to the oven until drying is complete.

See NAILS. **FINGER NAILS**

FISH

Fish needs to be very fresh to ensure an enjoyable meal. When buying fish, always look it straight in the eye and get close enough to assure yourself the slight sea smell remains. If clean eyes and a salty smell, then it's fresh.

To remove the smell of fish, see mustard.

FISH ROLL

All you need is about three cups of cold fish. Any fish will do, but make sure the bones are all out. Rub 2 dessertspoons Margarine into 1 cup Plain (All Purpose) Flour, add 1 teaspoon Salt and ½ teaspoon Pepper and 1 cup mashed Potatoes. Mix to a pastry-type consistency with 1 beaten Egg. If the consistency is a little thin, add a little more flour. Roll this mixture out on a floured board, spread the flaked fish over, roll up and place on a greased dish and bake until browned in a fairly hot oven. This can be sliced and served cold with salad or hot with vegetables. I usually add some chopped up parsley and a squeeze of lemon juice when I spread the fish, but this is a matter of taste.

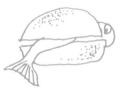

FLEAS

A plague of fleas can be very trying and very hard to get rid of. It is always a good idea to have mint growing, even if it is only in a pot on a verandah. Where you have an invasion of fleas, put mint under the mattress, sheets and mats, change it as often as possible, the fleas don't like it and you will get rid of them very easily.

FLOOR POLISH

To one tablespoon of Beeswax Floor Polish add a few shavings of any good household laundry soap and half-a-cup of Kerosene. Cover with sufficient boiling water to quarter fill a plastic bucket. Stir well and apply with a mop. Allow to dry, then rub with a dry mop.

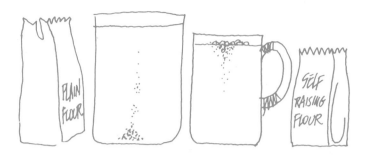

FLOUR If you are not sure what flour is in which container, a simple test is necessary. Add a teaspoon of flour to a glass of water. The Self-Raising Flour will bubble to the top. The Plain Flour (All Purpose) will not.

FLUFFY TOYS Because children love them so much, fluffy toys get soiled quickly. It is better to wash them but you need to be sure the stuffing is washable so colours will not run. If these points are uncertain, get a block of powder magnesia from the chemist or drug store and go over the toy with it. Leave for 20 minutes then give the toy a good spanking to get rid of the powder.

FRUIT CAKE DRY If a fruit cake is dry, change it into something else.

1. STEAMED PUDDING. Just crumble the cake, mix a beaten egg through it, put into a greased basin and steam for about half an hour. Serve with a custard sauce or icecream.

2. RUM BALLS. 2½ cups of fruit cake crumbs, 1 tablespoon rum, 60 grams (2 ozs.) melted copha, 1 tablespoon cocoa. Combine all ingredients and mix well, Shape into small walnut size balls and roll in crushed nuts or coconut. Chill until needed.
Push a knitting needle down through the cake almost to the bottom in a number of places and pour Brandy or Sherry down into the holes. Wrap it well in foil and let it sit for a while.

Most fruit will ripen easily if put in a brown paper bag with an apple.

If a pineapple is a little green, it can be ripened evenly by removing the leaves and standing it upside down in a paper bag.

FRUIT
To ripen

For home made Fruit Salts, mix 60 gms (2 ozs.) Tartaric Acid, 60 gms (2 ozs.) Bi-carbonate of Soda, 60 gms (2 ozs.) Cream of Tartar, 155 gms (5 ozs.) Castor Sugar, and 30 gms (1 oz.) Epsom Salts. Mix well then bottle and store in a dry place. Use 1 teaspoon to a glass of water.

FRUIT SALTS

Most fruit stains can be removed by covering the stain with Borax then let hot tap water run through it.

FRUIT STAINS

The bottom of electric frypans sometimes blacken. To prevent this, stand the frypan on three layers of newspaper while cooking. If it has blackened, turn it upside down and cover the bottom with a cloth dipped in Cloudy Ammonia. Leave overnight, then wash normally.

FRYPAN

Never store furs in a plastic bag. Make up a muslin bag and add to it a few herbs such as rosemary, verbina, a cinnamon stick and a few cloves to discourage the moths. A calico bag is also good for storing furs in.

FUR

For furs which may have developed a musty smell, use a packet of rolled oats. Heat the oats in the oven until they are just warm to touch, take them out and sprinkle a full bottle of Nilodor over them. The coat should then be placed flat and covered completely with the warm rolled oats. Rub gently into the fur, leave for about an hour, then hang outside to air. This will brighten up the fur as well as removing any odour.

White fur can be cleaned and freshened by warming a few cupfuls of flour in the oven, and then sprinkling it over the coat. Rub in with the hands. Leave for about an hour, then shake out thoroughly. A good beating will not harm the fur and will get all the flour out.

FURNITURE For white heat marks on wooden furniture, rub with cigarette ash made into a paste with a little water, or rub with Brasso. Another method is to rub gently with camphorated oil. Marks from glasses or vases can be treated the same way. Teak can be treated this way, but only use teak oil to polish.

FURNITURE
Fading Tables, chairs, desks and other items featuring wood, need special care to prevent fading. Mix equal parts of boiled linseed oil, methylated spirits (U.S.A. — Solox) and brown vinegar. Rub with the grain using a soft cloth, then use a very light polish.

FURNITURE
Carved Carved furniture is very beautiful, but difficult to dust. An old shaving brush is good, but as so many men use electric razors today, it may be a good idea to look for a baby's very soft hair brush. Use a little cedar oil to bring up the polish. Never put polish directly on to the wood. Always put polish on to a cloth and rub with the grain.

FURNITURE
POLISH Equal parts of mineral turpentine, vinegar and raw linseed oil. Apply with a soft cloth.

FURNITURE
Freshener Sometimes furniture gets a slightly tired smell, particularly if you have pets and children. Freshen upholstered furniture by wiping all the seams and crevices with a cloth that has been dipped in warm water, wrung out until almost completely dry, then sprinkled with a few drops of Nilodor. This will freshen the room completely.

GARDEN SPRAY

In a bucket of water, put a small packet of Epsom Salts and 1 teaspoon of Condy's Crystals (obtainable from chemists or drug stores). Use as a garden spray for plants, shrubs and vegetables.

GARLIC SPRAY. Four hot peppers, four big onions, 2 bulbs of garlic. Crush and cover with water, leave up to 24 hours. Strain, and add water to make up to 4 litres.

These sprays are non-toxic.

GARLIC PASTE

Put 4 to 6 cloves through a garlic crush, moisten with a little olive oil and mix to a paste. Put the mixture into jars, cover with clarified butter and store in the refrigerator.

GARLIC POWDER

When bulbs are dry, peel and put through a mincer or food processor. Save the juice and use it to flavour some of the dishes that you are making in the next few days. Dry the minced garlic in the oven, using the lowest setting possible, and leaving the oven door just ajar. When it is dry, grind into a powder. It takes a lot of bulbs to make a little powder, so you may prefer to add the powder to salt and have garlic salt instead.

GENTIAN VIOLET

On clothing or carpet, use calomine lotion, or, dab gently with Methylated Spirits (U.S.A. — Solox).

GHEE

Ghee is the Indian name for clarified butter, made in India from buffalo's milk, and in western countries from cow's milk.

As a cooking medium ghee's value is high. When boiling, it is perfectly still and there is no spluttering, It does not burn or blacken when used for frying.

GINGER BEER

It is preferable to use a stone crock but any jar large enough to hold about 4 litres (2 gallons) will do. Into the jar, put 1 small cup warm water, 1 dessertspoon sugar, 1 teaspoon ground ginger, 2 teaspoons compressed yeast dissolved in a little warm water. Let it all stand for 24 hours. This is the 'plant'. After 24 hours, mix 1 small cup of sugar, 1 teaspoon ground ginger, 1 cut up lemon, without the white pith. Add enough hot water to dissolve the sugar, add cold water to make it lukewarm, then pour onto the plant. Then fill the jar right up, and leave for another 24 hours. Strain off through muslin, bottle and cork tightly. We used to tie the corks down with string, but screw tops will be satisfactory if put on with a very firm hand.

Now make up another mixture the same as you did after the first 24 hours, and pour over the plant.

Never leave the plant without adding to it, for more than 24 hours. If the plant gets too hot it may be divided or thrown out. Never have more than 6mm (¼") to 12mm (½") of plant in the jar. Make sure you have plenty of thoroughly clean bottles before you start.

GINGER Chinese

For thousands of years the Chinese have been aware of ginger as an aid to digestion, which is why it is included in so many of their dishes. It adds flavour and helps to digest spicy foods. A good idea is to use it instead of After Dinner Mints.

I always think Ginger Marmalade is a good sharp start to the day! It is also simple to make. Chop 500 grams (1 lb.) grapefruit finely and pour one litre of cold water over it. Next day, boil the water and fruit together for about one hour. Add 1½ kilos (3 lbs.) of sugar and 1 teaspoon Powdered Ginger. Boil for about 45 minutes, or until it sets when tested. Just before turning into sterilized jars, add 15 grams (½ oz.) of finely chopped Preserved Ginger and stir well.

When cleaning mirrors or windows, a mixture of equal parts water, kerosene, methylated spirits (U.S.A. = Solox) and cloudy ammonia is good. After rubbing on the mixture, polish with a soft dry cloth.

CLOUDY GLASSES. Drinking glasses sometimes go cloudy, particularly if a dishwasher is used. If this occurs, wash them by hand in hot soapy water with a little Cloudy Ammonia in the water. Sometimes it is a good idea to crush some egg shells in each glass and shake well. Another method is a little salt and vinegar rubbed around the glass with the dishwashing sponge, then rinse well in hot clear water.

GLASS

Many of the new plastic based glues cannot be removed from fabric without ruining the garment and the only hope is to remove as much as possible before the glue sets.

Eucalyptus will remove some types of glue from clothing. Put Eucalyptus on a pad and hold on the stain. If your fingers are stuck together with glue, just pour some eucalyptus over them, rub firmly and the glue will come away quite easily.

Some residual glue marks particularly those which are tacky to touch, can be removed with a product called Zoff, obtainable from chemists or drug stores.

GLUE

See JEWELLERY.

GOLD

When properly preserved, gourds make a most attractive table decoration. Make sure you pick them from the vines when ripe, and leave a short stem attached. Allow them to dry in the sun, but if that is not possible, dry out in the oven, with the door left slightly open. When completely dry, spray with a clear laquer. Gourds are ripe when the stem behind the fruit begins to dry.

GOURDS

GRASS STAINS Clean grass stains as soon as possible. If the material is cotton, use 2 parts methylated spirits (U.S.A. = Solox) to 1 part cloudy ammonia and three parts hot water. Soak in this mixture before washing.

For knitted fabrics, dampen the stain, cover with toothpaste. Leave 20 minutes, then rinse the toothpaste away with warm water.

For synthetic fabrics, spray with Nifti. Leave 20 minutes, then wash the garment in the normal way.

GRAVY A skin forming on gravy spoils the appearance. To prevent this, take the pan off the heat, add a little melted butter and stir well, the skin will then come away.

Lumpy gravy is also a problem. Always add hot liquid to the flour very slowly and stir to keep it off the boil. Should it lump, beat with a hard whisk, or strain before using.

GREASE On carpet Cover with talcum powder to absorb the grease. After the powder, test the amount of grease left by putting three layers of brown paper over the stain, and holding a hot iron over it. DO NOT PRESS DOWN. As the paper absorbs the grease, change to a clean piece. Then sponge with a good carpet cleaner. Don't get the carpet too wet, and always mop excess water immediately.

GREASE On clothing Put the garment flat and smother with talcum powder. Leave the talcum powder for at least an hour and then remove. Now cover with powder again and put a couple of layers of paper towel underneath the greasy mark and more paper towel over the top of the powder. Now hold a hot iron over the paper, but do not press down onto the garment. The heat will draw the greasy mark up into the powder and you will be able to shake it off and lightly sponge any residual mark with eucalyptus.

On concrete, use one part detergent to six parts kerosene, leave five minutes and hose.

GREASE
On concrete

Try soda while it is still fizzing (see Suede), or pack with a mixture of 2 tablespoons Borax, 1 tablespoon salt and 2 teaspoons dry cleaning fluid. Leave for 24 hours, then brush off.

GREASE
On suede

Greasy overalls can be difficult to wash. One way is to add a tablespoon of bi-carbonate soda to the washing powder, or put a handful of salt in the washing machine.

GREASY
OVERALLS

Never add bi-carbonate soda to green vegetables when cooking. It is better to use a small knob of dripping, which keeps the vegetables looking green, and stops the water from boiling over.

GREEN
VEGETABLES

Soap residue collects on grouting and to clean it off, use a small nailbrush. If the grouting is white, use bleach. If the grouting is coloured, use Epsom Salts on a Soft, wet brush.

GROUTING

71

GRUBS This term covers a multitude of things, all of them nasty. Whether indoors or outdoors, on plants or on flowers, any grub should be identified, so that it may be treated with the right thing. The best thing to do is to take a sample of the grub to your nurseryman. In most instances he will be able to identify the grub and supply a spray or powder to combat it.

Gum Arabic Powder is available from any artists' supplies shop. To 1 litre of boiling water add 125 grams (4 oz.) Gum Arabic Powder. Stir until the gum melts, then strain through a piece of muslin. Bottle, cork and store for use later. For an average proportion, use 1 tablespoon of Gum Arabic Water to 1 cupful of water. This can vary according to the stiffness desired.

GUM ARABIC WATER

Guava fruit comes from a small tropical American tree. It is a rather pretty shrub and the fruit is either yellow or red. Guava fruit is ideal for making jellies, jams tarts and pies.

GUAVA

GUAVA JAM
Peel and slice fruit, discarding seeds. Boil skins and seeds in a very small quantity of water, enough to keep from burning. Strain and add to the sliced fruit. Add sugar in proportions of 1½ kilos (3 lbs) of sugar to 2 kilos (1 lb) of sliced fruit. Boil until set.

GUAVA MERINGUE TART
Cook a short pastry case and allow to cool. For the filling, cut up enough red guavas to fill the tart case, then boil 1 cup of water and three-quarters of a cup of sugar for a few minutes and thicken with a large tablespoon of arrowroot. Pour this mixture over the sliced guavas. Pour the mixture into the case.

Topping – beat two egg-whites stiffly then add one good half cup of sugar. Spread meringue over the top of filling. Bake in slow oven until lightly brown.

Guava Wine...

4 Kilos of guavas
9 Litres of water
1 Handful of raisins
1½ Kilos of white sugar to
each 4½ litres of juice

Boil raisins in the water and pour while boiling over the fruit. Let stand for 48 hours. Strain, add 1½ Kilos of sugar for each 4½ litres of liquor. Pour into kegs till fermenting has finished.

This takes about six weeks

Then bottle and SEAL...

If hairs from animals are left on chairs or carpet, wipe over with a sponge moistened with a little vinegar and water. This will pick up the hairs.

HAIR

To clean a hairbrush, use warm soapy water with a little Cloudy Ammonia. If the hairbrush has a wooden back, smear the back of the brush with Vaseline before washing. When the brush is clean, rinse and wipe the Vaseline off the back. Shake the water out of the bristles and run under a cold tap. Shake again and leave to dry.

HAIRBRUSH

To clean little girls' hair ribbons, wash in warm soapy water or Woolmix and wind the washed ribbon around a bottle filled with warm water. The ribbons will dry in no time and will not need ironing.

HAIR RIBBONS

Hairspray has more uses than was intended by the manufacturers. It holds the petals of flowers, extending their life. It also takes ballpoint ink off vinyl.

HAIRSPRAY

Once a ham is cut, remove the outer plastic covering and wrap it in a damp cloth. Change the cloth every few days. This should keep the ham fresh for at least three weeks.

HAM

HANDBAGS

For BEADED BAGS use powdered Borax. Rub the Borax into the handbag and leave for at least an hour then brush and shake out.

CANVAS bags may be washed and scrubbed with warm soapy water. To avoid mildew forming, make sure the bag is dry before storing.

For FABRIC handbags, use a powder carpet cleaner.

Clean LEATHER handbags with a soft cloth dipped in warm water to which has been added a little cloudy ammonia. When thoroughly dry, polish with a good cream, then spray with Tuxan Silicone Water Repellent. Don't use coloured polish on handbags as it is liable to come off on clothing.

LINING should be brushed thoroughly and then rubbed with a rag dipped in dry cleaning fluid. Do not make it too wet as the inter-lining, as well as the skin, may be damaged. Dry with a hair dryer.

PATENT LEATHER can look like new if polished up with Vaseline and then thoroughly rubbed off with a good soft cloth.

VINYL can be washed in warm soapy water to which has been added a little cloudy ammonia. Polish with a cream-type furniture polish.

HAND CREAM   If you have a sensitive or freckled skin, this hand lotion may help. Steam 10 large cupfuls of Elderberry flowers with 2 tablespoons of water for about 5 minutes. Add 250 grams (8 ozs.) of Vaseline and simmer for about half-an-hour. Remove from the heat and strain through muslin into jars.

HAND BASIN   See BATH.

To clean perspiration stains on the inside edge of a hat, rub with eucalyptus, or soap and a few drops of cloudy ammonia. **HATS**

To cook in a haybox you will need a box with a well-fitting lid. **HAYBOX** Line the box very thickly with newspapers, then fill the box with hay, packing very tightly until it is 13 to 15 cm (5 or 6 inches) thick all round. The corners must be well packed. Make nests for the saucepans, which must have tight-fitting lids to keep the steam in. A cushion of hay will be needed to cover the saucepan Finally, tuck in with an old blanket and close the lid of the box firmly. Food will not be over-cooked in a haybox, and may be left all day or overnight. It is important to start the cooking on the stove before putting it into the box, and sometimes the food may need re-heating, just a little, after taking it out. Delicious flavour!

TIME EXAMPLES: Porridge should be boiled for 5 minutes on the stove and spend all night in the haybox. Stew should be boiled for 20 or 30 minutes on the stove, then spend 6 or more hours in the haybox. Haricot or Navy Beans, boil 20 minutes on the stove then 1½ to 2 hours in the haybox. Potatoes, 5 minutes on the stove and 1½ to 2 hours in the haybox. Steamed Pudding, 45 to 60 minutes on the stove, 2 to 3 hours in the haybox. Experience will teach a great deal more as you experiment.

Heat marks on wooden furniture can frequently be removed by **HEAT MARKS** rubbing well with Brasso and then polishing with a soft dry cloth. Another method is to make a paste of cigarette ash and water and rub this over the mark. Always rub with the grain of the wood.

Skirts will go up and down with fashion trends. If you are letting **HEM-LINE** the hem down, to remove the line, just rub it with white vinegar. Then wring out a cloth in cloudy ammonia and a little water, and press over the cloth along the line on both sides.

HERBS
Fresh

To retain the flavour, stand fresh herbs in a glass with a little Olive Oil for a few minutes before putting them in a plastic bag in the refrigerator.

HERBS
To keep

Mint and Parsley die off from time to time, so when plentiful, pick and preserve, Parsley can be chopped and frozen. Remove stalks first. It separates easily when frozen, so it can be stored in a freezer bag and used as required. Parsley can also be dried, either chopped or in whole sprigs, by boiling it for a few minutes in a pot of water, then drying it fairly quickly in the oven. Before using, it is a good idea to soak the parsley in warm water for a few minutes to freshen it. To dry Mint, gather it on a dry day and dry it slowly in a very low oven. Crumble it when it is completely dry and store in airtight jars.

HERBS
Winter

The best winter herbs are Dill, Borage and Chervil. Sow these herbs in the autumn and there will be plenty of supplies for winter soups and casseroles.

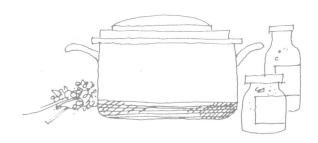

Holland Blinds, particularly those over kitchen sinks, often become water marked and discoloured. Water marks are almost impossible to remove. A good idea is to try to invert the blind, by putting the top to the bottom.

HOLLAND BLINDS

If this cannot be done, hot soapy water and a little cloudy ammonia often helps.

To measure honey, treacle or syrup, grease the cup or spoon first. It will pour more easily and will not be wasted by sticking to the surface of the measure.

HONEY

Cut thinly 125 grams (4 ozs.) of yellow soap into a double saucepan, occasionally stirring until it is melted. Keep it over the double boiler and add 1 tablespoon of Palm Oil and 1 table-spoon of honey. Then add a few drops of Oil of Cinnamon. Let it all boil together another 6 or 8 minutes, then pour out and let it stand. Cut up and it is ready for immediate use.

HONEY SOAP

Sauce made from horse radish is very hot and ideal for use with steaks or roast beef. Horse radish is easy to grow.

HORSE RADISH

A quick easy sauce to make is to 1 cup of white sauce add a pinch each of mustard powder, salt and sugar. Also 2 teaspoons of lemon juice and a tablespoon of cream. Then add 2 tablespoons of freshly grated horse radish.

TO KEEP, stand the stems of the hydrangeas in one-third glycerine to two-thirds water and leave for at least five days. Top up each day with water as it evaporates.

HYDRANGEAS

"Wool Mix is busier than ever in the warm weather."

"*I* suppose that because we associate woollens with Winter we tend to think of Wool Mix as only a Winter product. But my goodness, when the cold weather is past, what better time to give our heavy blankets and eiderdowns and continental quilts a wash and freshen up. Use Wool Mix and you'll be delighted with the results. The same goes for our Winter woollies. Spring is a wonderful time to remove any stains before they worsen and become difficult to clean. Then next Winter, when you take out your jumpers and cardigans, you'll find them soft and springy like new.

Of course, Wool Mix is ideal for many Summer uses as well. You know how sea salt can make your beach towels hard and rough. Wool Mix restores their softness and springiness. And it does the same for your tracksuit and any other terry towelling wear. Curtains really brighten up a room. But they do attract the dirt. Unlined terylene and other synthetic curtains come up like new in Wool Mix.

Look around the house and you'll discover new uses for Wool Mix all the time.

COUNTRY HOMESTEAD

Eucalyptus

WOOL MIX

"I recommend this no-rinse wool mix for a lovely soft wash for woollens"

750ml

Ice blocks will freeze more quickly if you fill the tray with warm water, not cold. It sounds strange, but it does work.

Heavy waxed paper, the type that you get inside breakfast cereals, can be placed under ice cube trays to make them slide in and out easily.

ICE

Just for a change, try making your own ice cream. Whip 1½ cups cream with ⅔ cup sugar. Add 1 cup milk, beat 2 egg whites very stiffly with 1 teaspoon vanilla and add this to the cream and sugar. Freeze. This is usually ready to serve in about 2 hours.

ICE CREAM

To remove the labels from ice cream containers, first soak them and get the paper off. The sticky adhesive that remains can be removed with Zoff, available from chemists or drug stores. Make sure the lid is thoroughly washed with hot soapy water before using.

ICE CREAM CONTAINERS

On furniture, sponge with a cloth wrung out in very hot water. When dry, sponge with dry cleaning fluid. If very obstinate, sponge again with luke warm water and Woolmix. Wipe clean with a soft dry cloth.

ON CLOTHING, sponge with fairly hot water and any good detergent.

ICE CREAM STAINS

Before icing a cake, brush over with white of egg. This prevents white icing from absorbing the colour from the cake.

To soften hard icing, very lightly brush with Glycerine. Leave for two or three days.

Avoid sticky icing by crushing a junket tablet into the icing when mixing.

ICING

INDOOR PLANTS

Indoor plants are very decorative, but need looking after. Just one rule – only water them when dry. Your thumb is the best judge of this and don't polish the leaves with oil, it could burn them. Use milk, about 1 teaspoon to a cup of water and the plants will be happier.

During the winter, ferns like a drink-daily diet because of the reduced humidity caused by heating. Try to keep any ferns well away from the direct source of heating whenever possible. An easy way to increase the humidity around indoor plants is to keep them sprayed with water.

INK STAINS

There are various methods to remove ink stains. Sometimes rubbing with a cut tomato and leaving overnight works. Or leave a handful of salt on the stain for a few hours. A subborn stain may need almost neat Cloudy Ammonia to remove it. The commercial product, Allandale Ink Remover, is quite good.

RED BIRO and RED TEXTA stains, try equal parts of Methylated Spirits (U.S.A. = Solox) and Vinegar. Dab the stain rather than rub it.

ON LEATHER. For ball point pens on leather, use Solyptol, sometimes Dettol works.

ON PLASTIC. It is very difficult to provide a stock answer as plastics have so many variables. Try milk first. Dab it on with a piece of cotton wool and rub over the stained area. If that doesn't work, try Methylated Spirits (U.S.A. = Solox).

PRINTERS' and some INDELIBLE INKS. Dissolve a dessertspoon of Oxalic acid, from the chemist or drug store, in about a breakfast cup of warm water. Put the stained part on a folded towel or cloth and dab with clean pieces of cotton wool dipped in the solution. Do not rub. When the stain has faded, rinse thoroughly with Baking Soda added to the rinsing water.

Photographers hypo is also worth a try.

Old-fashioned Citronella, available from chemists or drug stores, is very good to deter many insects.

It can be used either dabbed on face and hands, particularly for mosquitoes, or a few drops dabbed onto a tissue or piece of cotton wool will help to keep insects away.

INSECTS

Raw onion juice rubbed onto an insect bite will help to relieve the painful itch. Another method of relief is to rub the affected area with Methylated Spirits (U.S.A. = Solox).

INSECT BITES

Iodine stains can be treated by applying damp mustard over the stain. Leave for 24 hours, then wash in the usual way.

IODINE

The best Irish stew is made without water. Remember, a stew boiled is a stew spoiled. Put the potatoes, onions and meat into a basin, place the basin into a saucepan of slowly simmering water and leave for a couple of hours. This way you get all the natural juices and not a pot of watery meat.

IRISH STEW

To clean plastic film from the base of an electric iron, heat the iron and turn off the power. Then rub with dry steel wool and a little vinegar. If a little rust forms on the base, rub with fine wet and dry sandpaper. For Teflon coated iron, see TEFLON.

**IRON
To clean**

See CAST IRON.

**IRON
COOKING PANS**

IRONING Most people find ironing a very tedious task.

Don't iron more than is absolutely necessary. Fold sheets, towels, and flat articles as soon as they are dry and they will not need to be ironed.

Do have a good ironing board which is comfortable for you to use.

Don't have a highly coloured cover. Heat and steam could transfer some of the colour to the articles you are ironing.

Do use hot water to dampen articles to be ironed. Hot water penetrates better than cold.

A folded newspaper makes a good sleeve board as does a small cricket bat. Trousers should be ironed with a damp cloth over the knee area where stretching occurs. Always start ironing trousers at the knee.

IVORY HANDLES Never wash ivory in hot water. Ivory yellows with age, but hot water intensifies the yellow. If Ivory needs cleaning, rub well with powdered whiting and lemon juice.

To whiten knife handles, stand them in a glass of ½ water, ½ bleach for 12 hours. Then rub them with toothpaste. Dry and polish with talcum powder.

Fruit should always be gathered on a fine day, and it should never be over-ripe. Wipe the fruit with a damp cloth. Fruit should be partly cooked before sugar is added. Bring fruit to boiling point slowly to avoid burning. Always use a wooden spoon to stir jam. After sugar has been added, boil as rapidly as possible. Fast boiling improves colour and flavour of jam. To stop jam foaming while cooking, add a tablespoon of Brandy or a nob of butter. This saves skimming the surface. To test jam, put a little on a saucer. When it cools, a skin should form on the top. Jam jars must be thoroughly sterilised and thoroughly dry. Put jam into warm jars to avoid breakages.

Home-made jam cannot always be stored under perfect conditions, and we often find mould on the surface. Just before covering, and when the jam is quite cold, add a small teaspoon of vinegar to each pot then cover in the usual way.

JAM

Most jam stains will be readily removed by sponging with a solution made with half a litre (1 pint) of warm water to 30 gms. (1 oz.) of borax.

JAM STAINS

If jelly does not set well it is due to, either being overcooked, or the fruit is too ripe and therefore short of pectin. If this happens, use a commercial jam setter which can be purchased at supermarkets. The jelly may finish up slightly cloudy but at least it will not be wasted.

JELLY

JEWELLERY Jewellery can be cleaned by dipping it in a solution of warm water and cloudy ammonia. You may need a soft toothbrush to get in around the edges. Don't push too hard with the toothbrush or you could lose some gemstones.

Some people suggest gin for cleaning rings but this is expensive and cloudy ammonia is just as good.

GOLD PLATED Jewellery sometimes discolours. This is usually an indication that the gold plate has worn off. The only way to restore the plate is to have the piece re-dipped by a jeweller.

PURE GOLD sometimes turns black also. This is purely a chemical reaction which can often be cured by wearing a copper bracelet.

JEX See STEELWOOL

JUNKET Vary an ordinary junket by stirring in a teaspoonful of jelly crystals, any colour or flavour, and when the junket is cool, sprinkle the top with a few more of the crystals.

You can add cocoa or chocolate to junket to give variation.

If sediment has settled in a kettle, put in a cup of vinegar and one litre of water. Bring to the boil, then rinse well.

COPPER KETTLE. The outside can be cleaned with Worcestershire Sauce on a damp cloth. Buff up with a soft dry cloth. Another method is to use salt and lemon mixed to a paste and rubbed over the surface.

SEDIMENT can be prevented from forming in a kettle by adding one or two marbles to the kettle. The constant moving of the marbles stops the build-up of sediment.

KETTLE
To clean

Kerosene will sometimes remove mildew, particularly if the article is one to be washed.

Soak the mildew spots in kerosene, leave overnight and rinse the article the next day in warm soapy water. Kerosene on steel wool will often remove marks from linoleum. Wash over with warm water after you have treated the linoleum with the kerosene.

KEROSENE

The wick of a kerosene heater must be cleaned regularly. If it is not, nothing will stop it from smelling. Half-a-block of Camphor in the kerosene tank takes away the smell of the fumes.

**KEROSENE
HEATER**

Finding your front door key in the dark can be a problem. If you bore a hole off centre before putting it on the key ring, the key will stand out at an angle and is easily found.

KEYS

For breakfast, chop finely or mince a kidney. Beat an egg, add a little salt and pepper, then kidney. Pour in spoonful lots into hot smoking fat.

KIDNEYS

KITCHEN CARPET The type of carpet to use in a kitchen is that which is usually labelled Indoor/Outdoor Carpet. It can easily be cleaned by scrubbing with Woolmix.

KITTY LITTER Strange but true! Kitty Litter will clean concrete. Dampen the concrete. Spread the litter and scrub down with a yard broom.

KNITTING From a book belonging to my grandmother.

"We recommend our readers to attain perfection in this branch of handiwork, because, above all others, it is a resource to those who, from weak eyes, are precluded from many kinds of industrial amusements, or who, as invalids, cannot bear the fatigue of more elaborate work. The fact is that knitting does not require eyesight at all: and a very little practice ought to enable anyone to knit whilst reading, talking, or studying, quite as if the fingers were unemployed".

Watching television is a good time to knit but make sure you buy wool that is suitable for your needs. Always buy a little more than you need so that repairs may be effected in the future.

KNIVES A knife will sharpen more readily if it is thoroughly warmed prior to sharpening. To clean knives of stainless steel, polish up with Bon Ami fine cleanser.

Pearl handled knives should be washed in warm soapy water. Never in the dishwasher. Rub the handles with Vaseline, wipe off excess and polish up with talcum powder.

Ivory handle knives, refer IVORY HANDLES.

Bone handled knives can be treated the same as ivory, but they will not come as white as the ivory.

Labels, whether on a jar, or a registration sticker on a car, can sometimes feel as though they have been put on for life. Try a few simple ways of removing them, either by packing with newspaper soaked in eucalyptus, or a cloth with Shellite.

Another way is to warm up a little butter or margarine, put that on the label, and it will soon float off. For labels on furniture soak a cloth in eucalyptus, place it on the label, leave for about three minutes only, and the label should come away.

STICKY SUBSTANCE UNDER LABELS can be removed with Zoff, obtainable from chemists or drug stores.

PRINTED LABELS ON MATERIAL can be removed by sponging lightly with Methylated Spirits (U.S.A. = Solox). Then place face-downwards on paper towel, cover the back of the garment with a clean, dry cloth and press with a steam iron.

LABELS

Don't iron directly onto lace as the point of the iron will often catch and tear it. Always cover with a cloth before ironing.

To keep lace looking crisp and fresh it should be washed in GUM ARABIC WATER. From a shop which sells artist supplies, buy 125 grams (4 ozs.) of fine white gum arabic powder. Put it into a bowl and add one litre (2 pints) of boiling water. Stir with a wooden spoon until the gum melts, then strain through a piece of muslin, into a bottle, cork it and keep for use.

An average proportion for use is one tablespoon of gum water to one cupful of water, but this can vary according to the stiffness desired. It was always considered to be a superior starch for fine lace and crochet.

LACE

LACQUER
To remove
From a hardware or paint store, get a good lacquer stripper. It should be painted on, then rubbed with a good firm bush. Clean down with Methylated Spirits (U.S.A. = Solox).

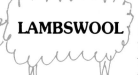

LAMBSWOOL
For lambswool trim on coats, etc., freshen up by rubbing vigorously with a cloth wrung out in Woolmix. Be sure to keep the moisture away from the rest of the coat. Dry as you go with a rough towel or hair dryer. See also SHEEPSKIN.

LAMINEX
Be careful when cleaning laminex that you do not scrape the surface. By using a weak bleach (one in four), most stains will come off. Toothpaste on a soft cloth also works. After cleaning, polish with a good car polish, or spray with Tuxan Silicone Water Repellent. Beeswax polish is also good.

LAMP SHADES
Lamp shades look attractive but they do collect dust and smoke. One of the safest ways of cleaning them is to rub with a dry shampoo. This saves getting watermarks on material shades.

Acrylic lamp shades can be washed with warm soapy water, then allowed to dry on a towel. Don't rub them as this increases static which attracts dirt. A bath is a good place for washing lamp shades.

Parchment lamp shades are best cleaned with a stiff paste made with starch and water. Allow it to dry and brush off.

LAVENDER
Pick the flowers before they fall and hang in a bunch, upside down in a dark place. When they're fully dried, skim the flowers free of the stalk, and to each two hundred and twenty-five grams of flowers, add fifteen grams of dried thyme and mint. Seven grams each of caraway seeds and a ground clove. Mix all together with fifteen grams of salt and put into bags.

The bags are good for perfuming drawers and wardrobes. Highly scented things are apt to keep moths away.

Leather absorbs grease and stains very quickly. So if a spot appears, clean it as soon as possible. Saddle soap or glycerine soap is safe on coloured leather. **LEATHER**

For a stubborn stain, pack with a mixture of 2 tablespoons borax, 1 tablespoon salt and 2 teaspoons of dry cleaning fluid. Leave 24 hours. Repeat if necessary.

To soften leather – boil ½ litre of linseed oil and allow it to cool. Then add ¼ litre of vinegar and rub into the leather with a soft cloth.

BOOKS which are bound with leather should not be kept in closed bookshelves as this encourages mildew growth. Always keep leather bound books on open shelves and dust regulary.

SCUFF MARKS can usually be removed by rubbing with an Indian Rubber, available from stationery shops.

WATER MARKS are very difficult to remove from leather. Brown vinegar on a soft cloth often works, or try Cloudy Ammonia.

Leeks are a good vegetable either served plainly boiled or with a white sauce. Don't throw away the green part as most of this can be used. **LEEKS**

Leeks also freeze well and are one of the few things that can be frozen without blanching, but do not keep them for more than two months in the freezer.

LEMONS A lemon tree gives a great deal for very little care. Whether in a big tub or in the ground, do grow one. We use them so much for cooking and cleaning. If they are in a tub, they will need a little more food and water than those in the garden. Be careful when planting, not to cover the graft.

To store lemons, always cut with a short stem and store in a dry cool place. Pack in sawdust or wrap in tissue. Rubbing with Vaseline helps to keep them.

To get more juice from each lemon, plunge them into hot water for 4-5 minutes or in the oven for a couple of minutes, or microwave for 15 seconds. Freeze lemon juice in ice cube containers and when solid, put the blocks into freezer bags.

EASY LEMON DRINKS. For cordial use: 6 lemons 30 grams (1 oz.) citric acid, 30 grams (1 oz.) of Epsom Salts, 1½ kilos (3 lbs.) of sugar and 1½ litres (3 pints) of water. Roughly cut the fruit and leave overnight in ½ the water. Next day, boil sugar and remaining water together. Mix all ingredients together. Strain and bottle.

Lemon Barley Water is most refreshing. Boil a cup of barley in plenty of water, strain, and to the liquid add the juice of 12 lemons, 10 tablespoons of sugar and 1½ litres (3 pints) of boiling water. You will be glad of a tree for this.

LEMONADE Boil 1 kilo (2 lbs.) of sugar, ½ litre (1 pint) of strained lemon juice until the sugar is dissolved. Pour the syrup out, and when it is cold put it into bottles, and cork closely. When wanted for use, put a tablespoon full into a tumbler three parts full of cold water. Stir in about ½ teaspoon of bicarbonate soda and drink during effervescence.

Plastic bags are a really great invention, but don't store leafy greens in them as they are liable to sweat and rot. Wrap greens in paper towels, then in plastic and keep in the vegetable compartment of the refrigerator. They will stay fresh and crisp for weeks.

LETTUCE

Instead of throwing away the outside leaves of lettuce, wash them, boil them up with some cucumber and any other vegetables you may have, even radishes, and put through the food processor. This makes very good soup served cold or as a base for hot soup.

Even with strict cleanliness it is still possible to pick up lice. Children frequently bring home lice eggs in their hair. The eggs, called nits, can of course be dropped onto clothing and carpet around the house.

LICE

Fresh air, sunshine and disinfectant are the remedies for lice. If they are in clothing, the clothes should be disinfected as much as possible, and put out into the air, preferably sunshine, turned inside out so that the air and sun can get to all the seams.

Kerosene is the general treatment of head lice, but many schools carry supplies of a shampoo for the treatment of head lice which is given freely. For the treatment of nits it is a good idea to wash the hair with vinegar and water and comb it through with a very fine comb. Chemists carry special combs for nits.

There are many gadgets you can use to remove lids but the cheapest and best is a piece of rubber from the surface of a table tennis bat. It makes a most effective grip. Buy one from any sports store.

LIDS – BOTTLE TOPS

Unless they are taken down, light fittings can be difficult to clean, because so often, the carpet underneath catches bits of grime and there's an additional job to be done. An easy way to prevent the pieces falling on the carpet, is to open and hang an old umbrella on the light fitting. The umbrella will catch any water and dirt, making cleaning less arduous.

LIGHT FITTINGS

LILY OF THE VALLEY In most old-fashioned gardens can be found a fragrant corner of Lily of the Valley. It can also be grown in a pot. Don't be disappointed if it does not flower in the first year. The pips from which they grow need to be at least three years old before producing a flower.

LILY PILLY JELLY Wash the lily pillys and just cover with cold water. Boil for 1 hour. Press the berries and strain. Measure the liquid and to each cup of juice add one cup of sugar and two teaspoons of lemon juice. Stir until the sugar is dissolved, then boil rapidly until the jelly sets when tested.

LILY POLLEN STAINS Pollen stains from tiger and other lilies can be removed by pressing a little tomato juice and pulp onto the stain. Leave for about half-an-hour, then wash. Another method is to soak with Glycerine and then wash.

LINEN Quite often when taking out linen that has been stored away, you will find small brown marks. These can usually be moved by rubbing them with baking soda and lemon juice before washing. If mildew shows, the fungus can be killed by putting it out in the sun or on the line on a frosty night or sponge with a weak bleach.

TO REMOVE THE DRESSING FROM LINEN, soak overnight in warm water with two or three tablespoons of Borax, then wash in the normal way.

TO STORE linen tablecloths, etc. roll rather than fold the article. If the articles are folded they will develop creases. Take them out every now and again and hang on the line to air. If they are to be folded again, fold off centre so that the creases are in a different place each time. If this is not done, the creases can set and be impossible to move later.

The best storage area for linen is a very dry area, with shelves or drawers lined with paper. Sprinkle Epsom Salts under the paper. This will deter moths and silverfish.

Mix together one cup Vinegar, one cup Turpentine, half-a-cup Raw Linseed Oil. Shake well and rub over the linoleum with a soft cloth, then polish with a clean cloth. Store this liquid in a bottle and shake well before use. **LINOLEUM To freshen**

Some wooden floors are polished with linseed oil which can build up, particularly around the edges. To remove the build-up, rub with a piece of old towelling dipped in a mixture of half Turpentine and half Brown Vinegar. **LINSEED OIL To remove**

Lipstick on material must not be rubbed as it spreads easily. Just dab with a good dry cleaning fluid, or put a little glycerine on the stain. Leave it a few hours and wipe with eucalyptus. **LIPSTICK**

1½ cups water, 1⅓ cups sugar, 1 tablespoon instant coffee. Boil and simmer for 30 minutes then add 1 teaspoon vanilla, 3 drops glycerine and 1 cup brandy. **LIQUEUR – COFFEE**

1 cup castor sugar, ½ cup water, ¾ cup brandy, 1 tablespoon glycerine and 2 teaspoons of peppermint essence. Green can be added for colouring if required. **LIQUEUR PEPPERMINT**

LIQUID PAPER   Mineral Turps is the only thing to remove Liquid Paper.

LIZARDSKIN   To clean lizardskin, sponge it with a few drops of Peroxide of Hydrogen, available from chemists or drug stores.

LOUNGE SUITE   It is always best to play safe when cleaning furniture covered in wool mixture fabrics. For velvet, use only a powder cleaner. Clean and freshen with a good foam cleaner or a powder cleaner. Powder cleaners are often easier to use.

LUREX   Gold and silver lurex and embroidery threads can be dry cleaned, but they sometimes become dull. To brighten them, sprinkle a little Cream of Tartar or Powdered Magnesia over, and gently rub with a soft brush. Shake the powder out and the silver and gold threads will look like new.

MARBLE To clean and freshen marble, rub with a cloth dipped in turpentine. Or if it is badly stained, use a paste made of chloride of lime and water. Beeswax polish gives a good surfce to marble.

For soft marble which seems to mark easily, treat the mark with powdered cuttlefish mixed to a paste with Methylated Spirits (U.S.A. = Solox). Rub in with the fingers or a soft cloth and when the mark has disappeared, polish up with a very good beeswax furniture polish. You may need to repeat this two or three times. If the mark is a coloured stain from claret, etc., add some bleach to the paste. Use about half quantity of Methylated Spirits and half bleach.

SMOKE-STAINED MARBLE can be rubbed over with a mixture of bleach and water. Use four parts water to one part bleach. Finish by polishing with beeswax.

MARCASITE Bracelets and brooches made of marcasite dull very quickly, especially if they are not being used. The best way to bring them to a bright shine is to rub firmly with soft tissue paper.

MARINADE Marinade usually has an acid liquid as a base with compatible addition of herbs, spices, sauces, etc. The marinade acts as a tenderizer, improves the palatability of older animal meats and acts as a pickle for a limited period if there is a high proportion of the acid liquid such as wine, beer, cider, vinegar, lemon juice.

MARINATE This means to immerse meat and let it soak in a marinade, or keep it constantly moistened for a given period of time.

MAJORAM See OREGANO

If marmalade won't set don't mess about trying to recitfy the mistake. Just get some commercial jam setter. You won't win a prize at the Show, but you will be saved much heartache and time. If it sets like toffee, just insert a sharp knife into the jar, add a little hot water and stir it around.

MARMALADE

For this recipe use any citrus fruit or any combination of citrus fruits. 500 grams (1 lb.) of fruit, one litre (2 pints) of water, 1½ kilos (3 lbs.) of sugar. Chop the fruit finely and leave overnight soaking in the water.

Next day boil the fruit for one hour. Then add the sugar and boil for about three-quarters of an hour, or until it sets easily.

MARMALADE

This can be used instead of discarding the fruit after juicing it. 2 cups of peel cut very finely, 8 cups of water, 2 medium lemons, 4 cups of sugar. Soak the peel overnight in the water, add the lemon juice and simmer with the lid on. When the fruit is soft add the sugar and boil until set.

ORANGE PEEL MARMALADE

MERCURO-CHROME Cover the stain with Calomine Lotion, allow it to dry, then brush off. Another method is to sponge the mercurochrome stain with equal quantities of Methylated Spirits (U.S.A. = Solox) and water. Then work Glycerine into the stain, wash in soapy water, and rinse.

MICE At certain times of the year mice will invade any house. If you can find where they are entering, and they have learned to ignore a trap, pack around their entrance with steelwool. Another way, is to sprinkle around cupboards and under the sink with oil of peppermint, or oil of cloves. Lots of highly scented talcum powder sometimes helps. Borax can also be effective as they don't like walking through it.

MICROWAVE Cooked food can be heated and served in just a few minutes in a microwave oven. For cooking, a good microwave cook book is essential.

You don't need a degree in engineering to use a microwave oven, BUT, you must take the time to read and understand a few basic rules. The most important rule is that metal is never put in a microwave. Read the instruction book and learn to enjoy microwave cooking. You will love it once you try.

You must kill the fungus in order to remove mildew. Hot sun will kill it. For white materials, use a weak bleach about one in four. On a dark material, sponge with Dettol. A paste of salt and lemon juice is good for delicate fabrics.

ON WALLPAPER, hold a folded towel over the spot with one hand, while you hold a heated iron over the towel with the other hand. Don't have the iron too hot as you will not want to mark the wallpaper. The towel will absorb any moisture from the mildewed area, and at the same time kill the mould. Any excess mildew can be brushed off. If any marks remain, rub over with bread which is two days old.

For stubborn stains ON CLOTHES, make a paste of powdered starch and water and pack over the stain. Leave until it is perfectly dry, redamp the stain and allow it to dry out again, preferably in the fresh air. Repeat this until the mildew marks have completely disappeared.

MILDEW

Milk boils over very easily. If you put a spoon in the saucepan this will prevent the mishap and the nasty smell of burnt milk.

If milk does boil over onto an electric element, turn if off immediately, then sprinkle liberally with salt. Leave it for a few minutes then wipe off with a damp cloth. This way the milk is cleaned up quickly and easily and the smell is completely obliterated.

MILK

For milk formula stains on flannelette and viyella baby clothes, try making a paste with equal parts of Borax, Cream of Tartar and water. Spread the paste over the stained area and leave it to dry. If the stain is still obvious, spray with Nifti, leave for 10 minutes then wash as normal.

ON MOTHERS' CLOTHES, the best method is to soak the garment in two tablespoons of Borax to one litre (2 pints) of warm water, for about an hour, then wash as normal.

MILK FORMULA STAINS

A little butter smeared under the lip will stop a milk jug from dripping onto the table.

MILK JUG DRIPPING

MOTH HOLES To repair moth holes, cut a small piece from the seam of the garment and stick onto the back of the hole with white of egg. Press with a warm iron, not too hot. It can also be stuck on with starch and cold water mixed to a paste, pressed with a hot iron, or with clear nail varnish.

MOTHER OF PEARL Should not be cleaned with hot soapy water. Much better to rub with a soft cloth which has been dipped in olive oil. Polish with silk. Another method is to rub over with Vaseline, then polish.

MOULD ON FURNITURE mould can be removed by sponging with a solution made from one teaspoon of Cloudy Ammonia to ¼ of a litre (½ pint) of hot water. Sponge over the mould patches and wipe dry very quickly.

IN BATHROOMS use bleach. 1 part bleach to 4 parts water, or one of the commercial mould removers.

See also MILDEW.

MULBERRY To remove a mulberry stain from clothing rub it well with a green mulberry then sponge off or wash normally.

MUSHROOMS To freeze mushrooms use only those which are fresh and undamaged. Trim across the base of the stem, and wipe with a damp cloth. Wash only if very gritty under gently running cold water and make sure they are fully dry. Blanch for two or three minutes and freeze. Field mushrooms which are open may be frozen without blanching.

MUSTARD
To remove
fish odour The smell of fish can be removed from a cooking utensil by sprinkling with dry mustard. Leave it for awhile then wash it in the normal way.

MUTTON Mutton is the meat of a mature sheep. The flesh is usually a deeper red than that of lamb. Mutton takes a little longer to cook and should be cooked slowly.

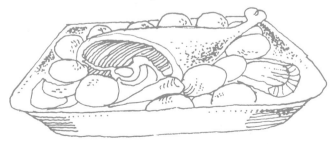

When hammering nails into hard wood, prevent bending by pushing the nails through a cake of soap before using them.

NAILS

STAINED FINGERNAILS can be cleaned by using equal parts of sugar, lemon juice and dripping.

NAIL BITERS should always carry an emery board in every pocket or purse. Little rough edges make such tantilising titbits.

Nail polish spilled on clothing or carpet can be removed with Enamel Solvent. Under no circumstances use nail polish remover as this will only spread the stain.

NAIL POLISH

Nail polish kept in the refrigerator will stay liquid and last longer.

To soften babies' nappies, soak for a few hours in warm water and Borax. Use about 2 tablespoons of Borax to 1 litre (2 pints) of water. After soaking the nappies, soak in Woolmix.

NAPPIES

Soak nappies overnight in cold water and Napisan. Next day, boil them for about half-an-hour in the Napisan. That should get rid of all stains.

NAPPIES Stained

For a larger crop of nectarines, plant a peach tree nearby. I'm told the bees love it and it works very well.

NECTARINES

For CARS or WARDROBES a few drops of Nilodor on a small piece of cotton wool will keep most odours at bay.

When cooking CAULIFLOWER or CABBAGE, put a slice of bread in the pot or a couple of slices of lemon. This will save the strong smell going through the house. Cooking in a little milk reduces the smell also.

The odour from CIGARETTE BUTTS can be quite offensive. If you find it so, put a bucket of water in the room with a few slices of lemon in it. This applies to the smell of fresh PAINT also. You need to change the lemons every couple of days. Burning a candle can be effective too.

MILK spilt in the car or on carpet should be sponged with Woolmix, dried, then sprinkled with a few drops of Nilodor. Another method is to make a paste with Cream of Tartar and cover the stained area. Leave it to dry and then brush off.

The smell of ONIONS cooking is really mouth-watering, but to remove the smell from your hands after peeling, rub baking power over palms and fingers, then rinse.

For PERSPIRATION ODOURS, see PERSPIRATION.

PLASTIC CONTAINERS should be washed thoroughly in plenty of hot water to which a little bleach has been added. Rinse, dry, and place in the deep freeze an hour or so before use.

In the REFRIGERATOR use a small saucer of dry mustard. Another method for the refrigerator is to use a small saucer or container of bicarbonate soda. Leave it in the refrigerator and replace every two months.

A spice which is very good used with poultry, fish, egg dishes, vegetable dishes and sauces. The pungency of oregano is better when dried and this herb is a popular ingredient on many regional dishes of other countries such as pastas, pizzas, etc.

OREGANO

Heat the oven. Turn it off and put a small bowl of cloudy ammonia on the middle shelf and a bowl of water on the bottom of the oven. Leave overnight and sponge in the morning with warm soapy water. The grease comes away quite easily.

OVEN
To clean

To clean the glass on the oven door, rub with a damp cloth dipped in baking soda. Then sponge with a clean soft cloth.

OVEN DOOR

Some over proof dishes can be used on the top of the stove either over a flame or on an electric hot plate, but if you are not certain, don't risk your oven proof dishes in this way. Should you wish to use them on the top of the stove use an asbestos mat.

OVEN PROOF
DISHES

If you have troubles with cakes rising too high and cracking across the top, it's a fair indication that the oven is too hot. It's a very good idea to have the thermostat tested.

OVEN
TEMPERATURES

Washing greasy overalls can be a problem. Wash them in the washing machine and add a handful of salt, or 1 tablespoon of baking soda to the detergent.

OVERALLS

OXTAIL Very good for soup or stew. A good stew is made with one oxtail, one carrot, one onion, one teaspoon of salt, one tablespoon of dripping. A bouquet garni, or flour cloves, one tablespoon of flour, one teaspoon of lemon juice.

METHOD: Cut tail into neat joints removing the fat. Roll in seasoned flour. Brown the sliced onions in heated dripping, meat and flour. Put meat, bouquet garni, lemon juice and onion in a saucepan, barely cover with cold water. Simmer until tender. This will take about three to four hours.

Remove bouquet garni and allow meat to cool. Remove the fat then add sliced carrot and simmer for about half an hour. If necessary thicken the gravy with extra blended flour.

OX-TONGUE Served hot or cold ox-tongue is a very pleasant dish but takes a little time to cook. To serve hot, boil one ox-tongue with one carrot, one onion, one clove, six peppercorns, one bay-leaf, half a sliced lemon and just enough water to cover all. Let it boil, and simmer for about three hours until the tongue is tender. Remove the skin and trim neatly, then strain and reduce the gravy.

Mix one tablespoon full of flour with 60 grams (2 oz) of butter and about half a litre (1 pint) of water or stock. When smooth and thick add the juice of half a lemon. Pour a little of the sauce into the dish with the tongue before serving. Some madeira wine added to the sauce makes this very delectable.

OYSTERS If you do not want to use oysters the day you buy them, they will stay quite fresh overnight in the refrigerator. Take them out of the shell and put into a container with a ¼ teaspoon of salt to 1 cup of water. The shells will also keep if you want to serve them in the shells.

PAINT

Get to paint stains as quickly as you can. On washable materials, use equal parts of mineral turps and cloudy ammonia and wash. If it is enamel paint, try a paint thinner. If in doubt, ask at your nearest paint store, they will help you.

Once it is dry, PLASTIC PAINT stains are almost impossible to remove. Dettol sometimes works, or ½ mineral turps and ½ cloudy ammonia.

There is a product on the market in Australia, called Lightning. It is available from hardware and paint stores. Although it has been designed for cleaning hands, I have found it very useful for removing some of the more difficult paint stains on clothing. Wring out a cloth in warm water, apply some Lightning to the cloth, then dab over the stained area. Afterwards wash with Woolmix.

TO REPAINT CANE, first strip existing paint off. As soon as the stripper has reacted and bubbled, wash it off with warm soapy water. Leave the surface for at least a week to make sure it is thoroughly dry before repainting.

PAINT SMELLS can be difficult to live with. An onion, sliced and left on a plate in a newly painted room with the window shut, will remove any smell of paint. Another method is to slice a couple of lemons and put them in a bucket of water and leave in the room overnight.

Before painting over an already painted surface, wash over with sugar soap, available from any paint or hardware store. Grease can be removed from a painted surface by rubbing with a slice of fresh bread.

PAINTINGS
To store The best way to store paintings is to hang them on a wall. If they must be stored, make sure the storage area is dry and airy so that mould will not occur. Don't stack paintings. Air should be allowed to circulate between them.

PAN FRYING Open pan flying often results in a lot of cleaning up from spattered fat. Next time, before beginning to fry, sprinkle cooking salt over the top of the stove. It absorbs fat spatters and prevents it from drying hard on the enamel.

PANCAKES Pancakes are useful for both sweet and savoury dishes. A good basic pancake recipe is one cup of flour, a quarter of a teaspoon of salt, one egg, one and a quarter cups of milk.

METHOD: Stir the flour and salt. Make a well in the centre. Drop in the egg and stir lightly, adding half the milk gradually, gathering the flour slowly. Beat with a wooden spoon until bubbles rise then add the remainder of the milk. Stand in a cool place for at least half an hour.

Heat a little dripping or oil in the pan. Drain off and pour in sufficient mixture (about two tablespoons) to thinly cover the bottom of the pan. Cook lightly until brown and set. Loosen the edges. Toss the pancake and cook the other side.

Serve either flat with lemon and sugar, or jam. Or roll with any savoury filling as required.

PANTIHOSE Pantihose will last longer by diluting one part mixed starch with 15 parts lukewarm water. Immerse the pantihose for 2 minutes. Remove, squeeze gently and dry. An invisible film then protects the pantihose and makes them last longer.

Old pantihose can be rolled into a ball to make good cleaning pads for the bath. Excellent because they don't scratch. Old pantihose are also good for buffing up furniture or shoes after polishing.

Wallpaper can be cleaned with slices of bread which is two days old. Cut it into pieces and make sure all the dust is blown from the paper which is to be cleaned. Wipe lightly over with the bread, discarding bread as it becomes dirty.

PAPER
To clean

Another method is to make a stiff dough with flour and water. Take a handful, knead it into a ball and carefully rub the paper, turning in the soiled portions of the dough from time to time and taking fresh pieces as required.

Clean with a handful of starch dissolved in a cup and a half of warm water. Rub the mixture into the shade with a sponge. Be sure not to get the sponge and the lampshade too wet. When the lampshade is clean, go over it with a damp sponge to remove the starch. If the lampshade is very dirty, use more starch in the mixture.

PARCHMENT
LAMPSHADES

To clean parquet floors, scatter with damp tea leaves then sweep thoroughly. If the floor needs a little more attention, mop over with a cloth which has been wrung out in warm water with a little kerosene added to the water. Don't get parquet floors too wet as water underneath will cause the parquet to lift.

PARQUETRY
FLOOR

Parsley stains can be removed by sponging with warm water and borax. Parsley can be washed, dried, chopped and frozen for continual use straight from the freezer.

PARSLEY

Parsnips are best steam blanched for freezing.
Scrub and peel, remove tips, then dice or slice. Water blanch for one minutes before freezing.

PARSNIPS

PASSIONFRUIT Passionfruit is best preserved by freezing. The fruit can be placed in the freezer straight from the vine. There is no need even to put them in freezer bags. Passionfruit will keep like this for at least twelve months and taste just as if freshly picked.

Another method is to remove the pulp from the skins. Put into icecube trays and freeze. When freezing is complete remove the cubes and put into freezer bags for storage.

The old fashioned method of preserving passionfruit using salicylic acid, is now frowned upon by health departments.

PASTRY Always obey the cardinal rule when making pastry. "Cool to make and hot to bake". Flour the board with cornflour and your pastry won't stick. When putting jam into pastry cases, warm the jam first to ensure crisp cases.

PATENT LEATHER To keep patent leather looking fresh and shiny, put a few drops of oil on a soft cloth and polish. That will remove greasy hand marks. Vaseline is good for patent leather. Rub on, then polish off.

Never store patent leather bags or shoes in plastic bags.

PAWPAW Seeds Save the seeds from fresh pawpaw and make salad dressing.

Put the seeds into a blender or food processor with 1 tablespoon sugar, 1 teaspoon prepared mustard, 1 teaspoon horseradish sauce, 1 cup salad oil, ½ cup brown vinegar and 1 small brown onion. Blend all together and keep in a jar in the refrigerator.

To clean and freshen peacock feathers which are used for decoration, use Woolmix with the peacock feathers lying flat in the bath. Gently ripple the water with your hands to loosen any dirt, then release the water and replace with rinsing water. Both the rinsing and the washing water should be warm, not hot.

PEACOCK FEATHERS

After rinsing, allow the feathers to dry completely. This will take approximately twenty-four hours, then gently shake the feathers before rearranging.

Make your own if your have a blender.

PEANUT BUTTER

Place ¼ kilo (½ lb) of shelled, roasted or salted peanuts, two tablespoons of peanut oil and, if the nuts are unsalted, ¾ teaspoon of salt, in the blender. Turn onto low speed until nuts are coarsely chopped. If crunchy style is wanted blend at high speed for half a minute.

For creamy style, blend on high speed for two minutes. Mixture will become firm on standing. This quantity makes about one cup of peanut butter.

If perfume is spilt on clothing, don't waste any time after discovering it. Rub in a little glycerine immediately, leave for a couple of hours, then wash in warm soapy water and rinse well. If the garment is non-washable sponge gently with warm water and borax.

PERFUME STAIN

Don't spray perfume when standing close to a polished timber dressing table. It is easy for the fine spray to get onto the timber surface. The spirit in the perfume will destroy the polished surface on the wood.

Beat together ½ cup Cream and ½ cup sof Cream Cheese. Fold into the beaten cream 1 cup ripe Persimmon Pulp and 1 dessertspoon Lemon Juice. Pile the mixture into a Short Pastry case and chill in the refrigerator. Serve cold.

PERSIMMON PIE

PERSPIRATION STAINS If you have bad perspiration stains or an odour that won't go away, sponge the stain with white vinegar. Then crush three Aspros with the equivalent of cream of tartar and mix with a little water. Leave on the stain for 20 minutes before washing.

For strong odours, hold over a basin of steaming hot water with 2 tablespoons of cloudy ammonia added.

PERSPEX Perspex is often used for record or cassette players. If the surface gets scratched, polish with Brasso.

PETS If the pets shed hair or fur on couches, chairs or carpets, dampen a cloth with water and a little vinegar and wipe it over. It will pick up the hair or fur very quickly.

For pets with a heavy animal smell, sprinkle a little old-fashioned Citronella around where they are sitting, similarly a few drops of Nilodor. Either one sprinkled on a cloth and left around where they sit is helpful.

PETROLEUM JELLY Many sportsmen use Petroleum Jelly to stop chafing. Some of it rubs off on clothing. Sponge the area with a clean cloth dipped in a little Kerosene. When washing clothes for a sportsman who uses Petroleum Jelly, add a little Kerosene to the washing water.

PEWTER To keep the lovely soft glow of pewter, polish regularly with powdered whiting mixed with a little oil. Wash pewter in warm water and Morning Fresh dishwashing liquid. Be sure to rinse in hot water, drain dry pewter mugs, and polish other articles with a soft cloth.

PIANO KEYS If piano keys are ivory, they will yellow over the years. Wiping them with methylated spirits (U.S.A. = Solox) helps. Also try and keep the lid open as much as possible.

If the keys are a composition, wipe with a warm soft cloth.

PICKLED ONIONS An easy recipe for pickling onions is as follows. Roll 1-1½ kilos (3 lbs) of peeled Onions in ½ cup of Sugar and ½ cup Salt. The easiest way is to put them all in a plastic bag and give them a good shake. Pack the spiced onions into sterilised jars. Add 2-3 cloves to each jar. Cover with vinegar. You will need about 2 litres (4 pints). Leave for 3 weeks before using.

PICTURE FRAMES To clean gilt picture frames, gently rub with bread which is two days old.

PICKLE This means to immerse in brine or vinegar solution, with or without herbs or spices, to preserve and add flavour to meats or vegetables.

PIKELETS

Quick and easy, pikelets can readily be made in an electric fry pan. You will need one and a half cups of flour, four level teaspoons cream of tartar, a pinch of salt, grated nutmeg if required, two tablespoons of sugar, two eggs, two level teaspoons bicarbonate soda, one cup of milk.

METHOD. Sift flour, salt, cream of tartar and nutmeg. Beat the eggs and sugar well then dissolve the soda in milk. Add flour etc. and milk alternately in two lots. Mix well. Cook immediately in dessertspoon lots on a hot greased surface. When the bubbles rise, turn with a broad knife or spatula and cook to a golden brown.

This recipe will make about forty pikelets.

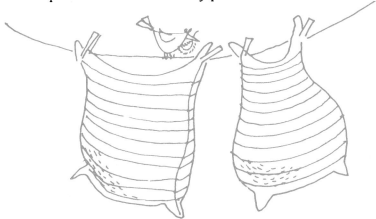

PILLOWS

Pillows filled with unwashable material can be lightly sponged with a cloth dipped in warm water and borax, or cleaned with powdered magnesia.

Feather down pillows can be washed in the same manner as a feather down quilt. In the washing machine with Woolmix, then tumble dry with a couple of clean tennis balls in the dryer. This will make sure the feathers are thoroughly spread, and the pillow comes out soft and fluffy.

Pillows which have seen their days indoors can be of continued use outdoors by making gay covers from one of the waterproof fabrics that are readily available today.

PIN FEATHER Trying to pluck a fine pin feather from a duck or gosling is very difficult. If you warm paraffin wax and allow it to set over the pin feathers, they will come away with the wax.

PINEAPPLE When you buy a pineapple, don't be put off if it is a bit green. You can ripen it by pulling out the top and turning it upside down. Store in a brown paper bag.

PLAIN FLOUR Australian Terminology for All Purpose Flour.

PLASTIC To sew plastic and prevent the material pulling and sticking, rub talcum powder liberally along the path you are going to machine. Lay a thin strip of paper between the seam as well. The paper pulls away quite easily when the sewing is completed.

PLASTIC CONTAINERS PLASTIC CONTAINERS should be washed thoroughly in plenty of hot water to which a little bleach has been added. Rinse, dry and place in the deep freeze an hour or so before use.

Many containers retain a smell after storing food in them. If this happens, put them in the freezer overnight or put a few pieces of charcoal in them and leave for a few days.

PLASTIC CUPS Clean with toothpaste or with Steradent tablets mixed with water.

PLAYDOUGH

So easy to get it into the carpet. Scrape off as much of the dough as you can, then sponge off with Cloudy Ammonia on a damp cloth.

A good way to keep children amused, particularly on a rainy day when they have to be indoors, is to let them make their own playdough. To do this they will need 1 sieve, 1 saucepan, 1 wooden spoon, and 1 wooden chopping board. The playdough needs 1 cup flour, ½ cup salt, 2 tablespoons cream of tartar, 1 cup water, 1 tablespoon vegetable oil, and a few drops of colouring. Sift flour, salt and cream of tartar into a saucepan, gradually stir in the water and oil until it is smooth. Add food colouring a few drops at a time, until it is a nice bright colour. Cook over medium heat, stirring continuously until the mixture comes away from the sides and forms a ball. This should not take more than two or three minutes. Remove from the heat and leave until luke warm. Knead the ball on the board until it is soft and pliable. Use an old chopping board as some of the colour may be transferred from the dough. Mould into any shape and leave to set. If left overnight the shape will become quite hard and could be painted over if necessary. To keep some of the playdough for another day wrap it tightly in plastic as it dries quickly when it is exposed to the air.

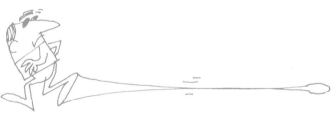

PLUMS

Pre-cooked and frozen, plums will last for about twelve months in the freezer. They make an ideal stand-by for pies or served simply as stewed fruit. Prepare and stew the fruit for about half the normal time.

To retain colour it is a good idea to add a crushed Vitamin C tablet to every half kilo of fruit.

POACH

Where a recipe calls for food to be poached, cook in liquid by simmering only. Do not boil.

POCKETS Before washing, turn pockets inside out and scrub along the seam with a nailbrush. This gets rid of any accumulated dirt. Patch pockets, on shirts particularly, always show a grubby stitch-line if not treated in this manner.

POLISH A good old fashioned polish is one cup turpentine, two cups linsed oil and one cup of water. It is necessary to give a good rub but it shines very well. Store the polish in a corked, well-labelled bottle.

POLISH BUILD UP ON FURNITURE To remove polish from furniture use brown vinegar. Wring out a cloth in warm water, dip in vinegar and sponge the furniture. Dry thoroughly before repolishing.

POMANDER See Pages 158 and 159.

POPCORN To pop corn, heat up a little oil in the bottom of a saucepan which is fairly large. Add the popcorn and put the lid tightly onto the saucepan. Hold over the flame and shake continually.

When the corn finishes popping remove from the flame.

To serve as a savoury with drinks, add melted butter to the popcorn while it is still hot, salt and pepper and some paprika.

PORK Roast pork is delicious, but should be kept moist. Put about an inch of water in the bottom of the baking dish, add the pork and do not baste.

For crisp crackling, rub in plain flour and salt and just before serving, turn the oven on to high for about 5 minutes.

POSSUMS

Possums are territorial creatures and, if they claim part of your territory, it can be very difficult to get rid of them, particularly if they claim the ceiling.

Naphthalene, lots of it, in the ceiling will help, particularly around the areas where they are getting in. It is much better to block the areas to prevent their entry.

Another thing which helps is quassia chips, obtainable from nurserymen. If you can get into the ceiling to clean it out before putting down the naphthalene or quassia, so much the better.

Scare-Away, a product used to deter birds from eating fruit. will also deter possums from eating plants. Just throw it over the plants that the possums like best.

POT POURRI

Gather the petals of all sweet-smelling flowers, such as roses, carnations, wallflowers, mignonettes, etc. and spread them out in the sun to dry. Whilst they are drying, sprinkle the petals with a mixture of 250 grams of salt and 7 grams of borax. A very light sprinkle is all that is necessary.

When the petals are thoroughly dry,50 grams of salt and 7 grams of borax. A very light sprinkle is all that is necessary.

When the petals are thoroughly dry, add up to twice as much lavender, a few bruised or Powdered Cloves, ½ teaspoon of Mixed Spice, ½ teaspoon of Cinnamon and a few drops of Attar of Roses. Mix it all together, and store in covered jars. For personal gifts, make into sachets.

POT ROAST

This is a method to cook a joint by first searing it on all sides, then adding 1 cup of stock or water, and when the liquid is reduced, add vegetables and cook with the lid on. Steam from the joint keeps it moist.

Ideal for less tender cuts of meat.

POTATOES

Some potatoes go watery when boiled. Don't panic. If you want to mash them, add a little powdered milk with the butter and they will soon thicken.

POTATO PEELERS should always be blue in colour. Blue does not resemble any fruit or vegetable and can easily be seen amongst the scraps and therefore not thrown out.

Store potatoes in a cool dry place. Never in a plastic bag. Potatoes are not so likely to turn green if kept in a tightly closed, brown paper bag.

POTTED MEAT For a different and inexpensive dish to make, try Potted Meat.

Cook 500 grams (1 lb.) of beef neck, cut into small pieces, in a little water for about 4 hours. This can be done on top of the stove or in the oven. Stand the stewed meat aside until the next day. Mince stewed meat two or three times. Season with Salt and Pepper, a little Mace, and Cayenne Pepper. Mix 125 grams (4 ozs.) of melted Butter in with the minced meat. Store in pots, covered with melted butter in the refrigerator.

POTTERY Some pottery vases are porous and can leak. If pottery vase leaks, dry it thoroughly and then give it a lining of the same wax you use for covering jam. Just melt the wax and coat the inside of the vase, using a small brush.

Another way is to paint the inside with a good lacquer.

POULTRY Any poultry or game is a good standby in the freezer, but BE WARNED – it cannot be emphasised too often – thaw whole birds completely in the refrigerator. They are particularly susceptible to bacterial growth which may not be destroyed in cooking if any part of the inside is still very cold, or partly frozen.

POUND Use a mortar, or a wooden spoon, to pound fresh herbs, etc., to a pulp. Use a meat mallet or rolling pin with vigour to tenderise meat by breaking down the tissue fibre and reducing thickness. To pulp minced meat, use a rolling pin with one handle sawn off.

Whole undamaged pumpkins, with a little of the stalk left on, will keep in a cool airy place for many months. **PUMPKIN**

All types will freeze but Butternut is best frozen. Peel, cut into service size pieces and water blanch for 3 minutes. It is better to puree older pumpkins for freezing.

Once a pumpkin is cut, the edge will need to be sealed in order to preserve it. This can be done by removing the seeds, sprinkling the cut edge with Plain Flour, or covering very tightly with plastic wrap.

To whisk root vegetables which have been boiled, steamed, or cooked in their jackets, do so with a little hot milk or cream, and melted butter, until smooth and creamy. Add extra seasoning to taste. **PUREE**

Cooked green-leafed vegetables should be very finely chopped or passed through a sieve before mixing with a little melted butter or cream, and adding freshly ground pepper. A little nutmeg improves the flavour.

DISHWASHING. WHO CARES?

USE HALF AS MUCH
AS OTHER LIQUIDS

MORNING FRESH

SUPERSTRENGTH
DISHWASHING LIQUID

500 ml

Cussons.

Morning Fresh is an extraordinary dishwashing liquid, as you'd expect from Cussons. It's super-strength, so you use only half as much. Which means it lasts twice as long.

Morning Fresh washes glasses, dishes, cutlery and pots and pans beautifully. And it contains a unique ingredient that actually helps clear away lingering cooking smells. Try it and you'll want to keep using it.

QUARRY TILES

Clean quarry tiles twice a year with equal parts spirits of salt and water.

Never use a fluffy mop or the tiles will smear. Remember to wear rubber gloves. If you should get a splash on your skin, treat it with vinegar.

Improve the look of unglazed quarry tiles by mopping over with a mixture of half Linseed Oil and half Turpentine. It's a good idea to wash the tiles first with hot soapy water and a little Cloudy Ammonia and allow it to be thoroughly dry before applying the linseed oil mixture.

QUASSIA CHIPS

Obtainable from nurserymen, quassia chips, spread about the roof and other areas where possums appear, will help to keep them away.

QUEEN CAKES

125 grams (4 ozs.) Self Raising (All Purpose) Flour, 60 grams (2 ozs.) plain flour, 125 grams (4 ozs.) butter, 125 grams (4 ozs.) sugar, 2 eggs, 2 tablespoons currants, a little candied peel, a few drops of vanilla essence, 1 or 2 tablespoons milk.

METHOD: Cream butter and sugar. Add eggs one at a time and beat well. Stir in fruit and flavouring. Sift in flour. Mix well, add milk. Turn into greased patty tins and bake in a moderate over 10 to 15 minutes.

QUILTS

Most quilts can be washed in Woolmix, but make sure you check the fabric of any quilt before laundering.

Feather quilts wash well in Woolmix, but add two clean tennis balls to the tumbler dryer whilst drying. This pushes the feathers around and allows the quilt to dry soft and fluffy.

QUINCE CONSERVE
3 kilos (6 lbs.) quinces, 3 kilos (6 lbs.) sugar. Peel and quarter the quinces, place in a pan and barely cover with water. Cook till soft. Lift fruit out into a basin and cover with a quarter of the sugar. Set aside for 12 hours.

Boil peelings and cores with the liquid from the cooked quinces for 1 hour. Strain and add the rest of the sugar. Bring to boil again, add quinces and boil till the syrup jells – about half an hour.

QUINCE AND RIPE TOMATO JAM
Peel and core 1 kilo (2 lbs.) of quinces and mince. Pour boiling water over 1½ kilos (3 lbs.) ripe tomatoes and remove skins. Put tomatoes and quinces in preserving pan with 2½ kilos (5 lbs.) sugar, and juice of 1 lemon. Boil about 2 hours but test often. Bottle when it sets. Delicious flavour, like rich raspberry jam.

If a rabbit is fresh, the body will be stiff, the flesh white and dry in appearance. Stale rabbits tend to be rather slimy with a bluish tinge to the flesh. The meat of rabbit is delicate but tends to be rather dry and is therefore best cooked with bacon to add a little fat to the meat.

RABBIT

Try growing radishes in pots, 4 pots is a good idea, with the seeds planted a week to 10 days apart. That way fresh radishes are available over a longer period.

RADISH

Strictly speaking, a ragout is a rich, highly flavoured sauce made with mushrooms, truffles, sweetbreads, stewed vegetables etc. and used as a garnish for entrees. Over the years ragout has simply come to mean, a highly flavoured preparation of meat, fish, poultry or game.

RAGOUT

Raspberry can stain quite badly. On washable materials first wash with soapy water, and then rub with lemon juice over the stain. Leave for about an hour before washing.

Of all the berry fruits, raspberries are the best to freeze. They retain colour and flavour exceptionally well.

RASPBERRY

RATTLING DOORS AND WINDOWS

Stick a strip of foam rubber around the area. This will stop the rattle and keep the draughts at bay.

Rats should be attended to by pest exterminators or contact your local Council. Prevention is better than cure so don't allow rubbish to accumulate and don't leave food scraps about. Rats can be very vicious if cornered so don't try to attack them yourself.

'RATS'

RED SPIDER MITE This generally appears on beans, and is at it's worst in hot dry weather, You will need to get a commercial spray for this problem.

REFREEZING Food which has been frozen then thawed should not be re-frozen UNLESS IT IS COOKED FIRST.

REFRIGERATOR The refrigerator will stay fresh and sweet smelling if you wipe it out regularly with vanilla. Also a good idea is to keep a saucer of mixed mustard on the lowest shelf. When moving house, pack the fridge with newspaper sprinkled with vanilla.

When defrosting, wipe the inside of the refrigerator out with a cloth wrung out in bleach. Use one part bleach to four parts water.

REGISTRATION STICKERS Kitchen plastic can be dipped in water and put over the registra-tion sticker. Leave it for a while and the sticker will move off the windscreen fairly easily. Wet newspaper also does the trick.

If you are figure conscious and enjoy rhubarb, cook in in Lo Cal Lemonade. Adding a little chopped apple and a dash of cherry brandy turns an everyday dish into an exotic tasty one.

RHUBARB

2 kilos (4 lbs.) rhubarb, 2 lemons, 500 grams (1 lb.) walnuts, ½ litre (1 pint) water, 2 oranges, 3 kilos (6 lbs.) brown sugar.

METHOD. Chop the rhubarb and boil in water for 20 minutes. Put oranges, lemons, and nuts through mincer, and add to cooked rhubarb. Add sugar and cook for about 1 hour, or until it sets when tested.

RHUBARB MARMALADE

Mix 2 cups chopped rhubarb with 2 cups sliced onion, 1 cup vinegar, 2 cups brown sugar, ½ teaspoon salt, cinnamon, ginger and cayenne to taste.

Put into an enamel saucepan, boil 20 to 30 minutes, or until the consistency of jam. Bottle and seal.

RHUBARB RELISH

RICE   To prevent rice becoming a gluey mess after cooking, heat a little oil in a saucepan. Then add the dry rice and shake it around so that all the grains are coated with the oil. Now add sufficient cold water to cook the rice with ½ teaspoon of vinegar and a little salt. Bring to the boil and when the rice is cooked, put into a strainer and run water from the hot tap over it.

If you cook too much rice, wrap the extra in foil and freeze it. It can be taken straight from the freezer to the oven for reheating. For reheating in a microwave oven use a plastic container not foil.

RICE PUDDING   Why not try old-fashioned Rice Pudding for dessert sometime. Put a scant cup of rice into 1½ litres (2-3 pint) of milk and let it stand for about 8 hours. Then add a piece of butter, about half the size of an egg, ¾ cup sugar, a pinch of salt, cinnamon or nutmeg. Bake very slowly for about 2½ hours at low temperature. After it has become hot enough to melt the butter, but not brown the top, stir it gently from the bottom, add a handful of raisins. Gently stir again and bake a little longer until the top slightly changes colour. This dish can be served with Golden Syrup or jam over the top of it, and with ice-cream if desired.

RINGS   To remove a tight ring from your finger, pass the end of a piece of fine string under the ring. Now wind it evenly around the finger upward as far as the middle joint. Then take the lower end of the string under the ring and slowly wind it upwards. The ring will gradually move along the string and come off.

Another method is to wet the finger, rub it with soap, then press the ring over the knuckle, turning it on the finger as you do so.

RISSOLES

If you are going to the trouble of making rissoles, make a good quantity and freeze them. Such a good standby if you are in a hurry.

A different recipe is ½ kilo (1 lb.) minced steak, 2 rashers of bacon chopped and gently fried with 1 chopped onion, a small knob of chopped green ginger. Allow to cool then add it to the minced steak with salt and pepper to taste, a dessertspoon of Soya Sauce, 1 tablespoon of Tomato Magic or tomato paste, a dash of Worcestershire sauce, 1 tablespoon of brown vinegar, the juice of ½ a lemon, 1 beaten egg, ½ teaspoon nutmeg, ½ teaspoon powdered cloves, 1 small tin of pineapple pieces and 2 slices of crumbled white bread. Mix all together well then roll in dessertspoon lots in flour and fry.

**ROAST –
To re-heat**

Sometimes, after a roast dinner, with plenty left on the joint of meat, you shudder at the thought of cold meat and salad and wish that you could have another roast meal. You can do this by soaking the joint for an hour in cold water before reheating in the oven. It will be just as juicy as if it had been freshly cooked.

ROSE

Roses will last longer if the bunch of roses when first cut, is put into a bucket of water. Then reach down under the water and snip the end of each rose, slitting up the stem a little as well. Leave them standing up to their necks in water for least an hour before arranging in vases.

Use a potato peeler to strip the ends of the stems of roses. Saves getting thorns in your fingers.

**ROSE PETAL
CHOCOLATES**

Remove the petals from the roses when they are just past the bud stage and beginning to open. Make sure they are dry. Dust them thoroughly with Icing Sugar, and with a pair of eyebrow tweezers dip each petal into melted chocolate. Add a few drops of Rose Food Esence, available from supermarkets, for extra delicacy to the flavour. A few drops of Glycerine added to the chocolate helps to keep it shiny. Spray a china plate or some other suitable flat dish with Pure and Simple, put the chocolate petals on it and allow to set. Serve as an alternative to After Dinner Mints.

I DON'T BELIEVE THIS..

ROSELLA CHUTNEY

This tropical fruit is not often available in the southern states of Australia.

4 cups of seeded rosellas, 1 red chilli, a garlic section, 1 small piece of ginger cut finely, 4 cups brown sugar, 1 teaspoon salt, 1½ cups brown vinegar, 2 individual size packets of raisins.

Brew vinegar, salt and sugar, and strain through a fine cloth. Add rosellas, raisins, and cook until thick. Add other ingredients and cook another ten minutes. Bottle and seal.

DID YOU KNOW ROSELLAS GROW FROM SEEDS...   *NO KIDDING!*

ROSEWOOD

Furniture made from rosewood should be rubbed every day with a clean soft cloth to retain its lustre. Polish only occasionally.

RUBBER STAINS

Many kitchen chairs have rubber stoppers on the legs. This is nice and silent, but they can mark your vinyl. The stains usually respond to treatment with a nail polish remover or Solvol Soap on a stiff brush.

RUBBER TREES

Under no circumstances should they be planted close to the house. Three to five metres is close enough to any structure. Rubber Trees are related to the Moreton Bay Fig, and they have a very large root system which can be damaging.

RUGS
Curling

If the corners of a rug or mat curl, sew or glue a small magnet or flat curtain weight on the offending corner. If a rug develops a fold or bubble in the middle, glue a strip of felt on the underside of the fold.

RUM BALLS

Crumble up about 2½ cups of fruit cake, add 1 tablespoon of Rum, or any other alcohol, about 60 grams (2 ozs.) melted Copha, and 1 tablespoon Cocoa (Carob Powder can be substituted for the Cocoa). Combine all the ingredients and mix well. Shape into small walnut-size balls and roll in crushed nuts or coconut. Chill until needed.

RUST

For rust in washable material, boil 1 teaspoon of cream of tartar in ½ litre (1 pint) of water and soak the stain. Bad stains will need lemon juice mixed with baking soda to remove them.

Rust on concrete can be removed with spirits of salts, but make sure you wear gloves.

Bleach will remove rust in some instances, but do not use bleach on coloured materials.

Rust build-up inside a kettle can be prevented by putting one or two marbles into the kettle.

A paste made with salt and lemon juice sometimes works. Leave it on the stain until the paste is dry. Brush off and repeat if necessary.

On woollens, try a paste made with Glycerine and yolk of egg. Leave for half-an-hour then wash off in luke warm water and Woolmix.

On silk, wash in warm water and Woolmix, then rinse. Then rub in plenty of dry Baking Soda and leave for 12 hours. Wash again in warm water and Woolmix.

Weights, Measures and Temperatures

All cup and spoon measurements are level; so do not use rounded cup and spoon quantities. An Australian Standard measuring cup and set of spoons is available from most home-maker stores and supermarkets.

LIQUID MEASURES

METRIC ml = millilitres	IMPERIAL oz = fluid ounce	CUP AND SPOON MEASUREMENTS
5ml		1 teaspoon
20ml		1 tablespoon
30ml	1oz	1 tablespoon plus 2 teaspoons
60ml	2oz	¼ cup
85ml	2½oz	⅓ cup
100ml	3oz	-
125ml	4oz	½ cup
150ml	5oz (¼ pint)	-
180ml	6oz	¾ cup
250ml	8oz	1 cup
300ml	10oz (½ pint)	1¼ cups
360ml	12oz	1½ cups
420ml	14oz	1¾ cups
500ml	16oz	2 cups
600ml	20oz (1 pint)	2½ cups

MASS MEASURES
(Meat, Poultry, Butter, Etc.)

METRIC g = grams kg = kilograms	IMPERIAL oz = ounces lb = pounds
15g	½oz
30g	1oz
60g	2oz
90g	3oz
125g	4oz (¼lb)
155g	5oz
185g	6oz
220g	7oz
250g	8oz (½lb)
280g	9oz
315g	10oz
345g	11oz
375g	12oz (¾lb)
410g	13oz
440g	14oz
470g	15oz
500g (0.5kg)	16oz (1lb)
750g	24oz (1½lb)
1000g (1kg)	32oz (2lb)
1.5kg	3lb
2kg	4lb

COOKING TEMPERATURES

DESCRIPTION	ELECTRICITY METRIC °C = degrees celcius	ELECTRICITY IMPERIAL °F = degrees fahrenheit	GAS METRIC °C = degrees celcius	GAS IMPERIAL °F = degrees fahrenheit
Plate warming	60°C	120°F	60°C	120°F
Keep warm	80°C	160°F	80°C	160°F
Cool	110°C	220°F	100°C	200°F
Very slow	120°C	240°F	120°C	220°F
Slow	150°C	325°F	150°C	300°F
Moderately slow	170°C	350°F	160°C	325°F
Moderate	200°C	375°F	180°C	350°F
Moderately hot	220°C	400°F	190°C	375°F
Hot	230°C	450°F	200°C	400°F
Very hot	250°C	500°F	230°C	450°F

LENGTH

METRIC mm = millimetres cm = centimetres	IMPERIAL in = inches
5mm	¼ in
10mm (1cm)	½ in
20mm (2cm)	¾ in
25mm (2.5cm)	1 in
5cm	2 in
8cm	3 in
10cm	4 in
12cm	5 in
15cm	6 in
18cm	7 in
20cm	8 in
23cm	9 in
25cm	10 in
28cm	11 in
30cm	12 in

A most aromatic herb which is very good with any meat dish. Often used in savoury omelettes

SAGE

A lovely crisp salad can be enjoyed all year round, but make sure it keeps crisp by inverting a saucer in the base of the bowl, the moisture will drain under the saucer.

**SALADS –
To keep crisp**

Wooden salad bowls should not be washed as a general rule. Wipe with kitchen paper before putting away. If a smell builds up which is unpleasant, wash the salad bowl in warm soapy water and wipe over with oil and vinegar.

SALAD BOWLS

2 teaspoons dry mustard, 1 dessertspoon butter, 1 tablespoon sugar, 2 dessertspoons vinegar, 1 egg, ¾ cup milk, ½ teaspoon salt.

**SALAD
DRESSING**

Put mustard, butter, sugar into a double saucepan, Stir until butter and sugar melt, then add beated egg and milk. Stir till well blended. Remove from heat, add vinegar and salt. Stir till mixture coats the spoon, like custard. Use a wooden spoon for stirring.

See also PAW PAW SEED DRESSING

SALT   In humid weather, salt gets quite lumpy. A little cornflour mixed with it will make it free flowing or, put a couple of navy beans in the bottom of the shaker.

OVER-SALTING. If you should put too much salt into a dish, peel a couple of potatoes and throw them into whatever you are cooking. They absorb the salt. Just before serving, remove the potatoes and throw them away.

SALT SUBSTITUTE. Herbs are a good substitute for salt in many dishes. Celery, Summery Savoury, Thyme and Marjoram are all salt substitutes.

SANDFLIES   A few dabs of citronella on the skin will help to keep sandflies at bay. If bitten, equal quantities of cold tea and methylated spirits will ease the itching almost immediately.

SANDWICHES   For variation in sandwich fillings, try some of the following –

Left-over green vegetables with chopped mint and mayonnaise.
Finely diced celery mixed with chopped apple and dates.
Cooked brain and cashew nuts with parsley and bacon.
Vegemite and chopped walnut.
Cheese and grated carrot.
Cheese and tomato sauce.
Tomato and egg.
Dates and walnuts.
Grated cheese and potato.

If sash cords have to be replaced, make sure that it is done with nylon cord which not rot. **SASH CORDS**

Stains on satin should always be removed with dry-cleaning fluid. Satin garments, such as old wedding dresses, should be entrusted only to a commercial cleaner who also redresses fabric. Satin made with synthetic fibres are usually washable. **SATIN**

Much depends on the type of saucepan to be cleaned and how badly it is burnt. A good general rule is to add about an inch of oil, bring it to the boil and rub with steelwool. Or cover the base with salt and a little water and put on a low heat, with the lid on, and the burn should peel off. **SAUCEPANS Burnt**

Treat enamel saucepans carefully as they can scratch. Boil Bicarbonate Soda with a little vinegar and then rub with a soft cloth.

For stainless steel saucepans, put in a large unpeeled onion, cover with water then bring to the boil, and leave till it cools.

To prevent a black rim on saucepans when boiling a pudding in a basin, put a few slices of lemon in the water. This applies at Christmas time when the puddings need long, slow cooking.

One troublefree way to get rid of burnt offering at the bottom of the saucepan, is to place the saucepan outside for a couple of weeks. Nature will do the work for you and the burnt part should peel off quite easily.

Other useful tips for burnt saucepans are –
Put some vinegar in, bring it to the boil, then leave to cook for half-an-hour with the lid on.

Half-fill with water and put in one or two onions cut up, skin and all. Boil for half-an-hour, then leave until the next day. Particularly good for aluminium.

If you have fowls, put the saucepan in the fowl-run with some milk in it. The fowls will peck it clean.

Put some ashes and a handful of washing soda in the saucepan, half-fill with water and boil with the lid on, then leave until it is cold.

SAUSAGES To prevent sausages from oozing out at either end whilst cooking, put them into water, bring to the boil, strain immediately, then cook in the normal manner. Sausages done like this freeze very readily and can be used direct from the freezer, either for the pan, or for barbeque cooking.

SAUTE Saute means to cook in an open pan in a small amount of hot oil, butter or fat. The fat should be free of moisture and, if necessary, clarified. Heat slowly at first to evaporate moisture and prevent spattering.

SAVORY Savory is a herb which grows from either cutting or by seed. The finely chopped or dried leaves go with all kinds of cooked beans, either sprinkled over the beans or with a little melted butter, or in a cream.

The fresh or dried herb can be mixed with breadcrumbs for coating fish, pork or veal fillets before frying. It is a good flavouring for seafood sauces and cocktails.

The best scones are made with sour milk or sour cream. Not only are they lighter and more fluffy, but the flavour is deliciously improved.

Scones freeze very well, but if you are unable to thaw them slowly for unexpected guests, put them in the frypan. Warm scones with jam and cream are delicious anyway.

An expert scone maker I know gives these tips –
Use Plain Flour and Baking Powder, not Self-Raising Flour.
Three teaspoons Baking Power to two cups flour.
Always use a knife to mix the dough, and do not mix more than is necessary.
Most important, sour milk for mixing.
If you don't have sour milk, mix a little lemon juice with it. That will sour it.

PLAIN SCONES: 2 cups self-raising flour, a pinch of salt, 2 teaspoons of butter, nearly 1 cup of milk.

Sift the flour and salt. Add butter and rub into flour. Add sufficient milk to make a soft dough. Turn onto a floured board and knead very lightly. Roll out to 2 cm (¾ inch) thick, cut into shape. Put on a hot floured tray and bake for 7-10 minutes in a very hot oven. Scones may be glazed by brushing over with milk before putting into the oven.

FRIED SCONES: 1 cup flour, 1 teaspoon baking powder, salt and milk to mix.

Mix ingredients into a soft dough. Roll out and cut into circles. Have the pan half full of very hot fat and fry until golden brown. Very good served with bacon and eggs for breakfast.

OATMEAL SCONES FROM LEFTOVER PORRIDGE:
Take cold porridge, flour, sugar and a little butter. Make a stiff dough by adding flour to the porridge and flavour with a few drops of vanilla essence. Roll out the dough to 1.3 cm thick, cut into shapes, and bake for about ½ hour in a moderate oven.

Cut open, spread with butter, and sprinkle with raw sugar. Currants may be added to this mixture.

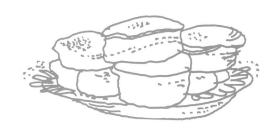

SCORCH Make sure the mark is only a scorch and not a burn mark. A scorch you can move by rubbing with dry steelwool to remove surface brown, and if a pale-coloured material, sponge with a weak bleach about 1 part in four. On a silky synthetic, make a paste of glycerine and borax and leave it to dry before brushing off. This can be used if you worried about the colour of the material.

Some scorch marks can be removed with a 50-50 solution of hydrogen peroxide and water. Don't leave it soaking, do it quickly, then wash the garment thoroughly. With this method, it is always necessary to test the fabric on a seam which will not show. Remember, if in doubt, don't.

ON DENIM, pack the scorched area with a paste made with equal parts of Cream of Tartar, Borax and water. Allow to dry and brush off.

SCRATCHES On varnished furniture, scratches may be removed by placing a coarse cloth well soaked in linseed oil on the scratches. Leave for a short time, rub a little, then remove excess, and polish. Deeper scratches can often be covered by applying a little shoe polish the same colour as the furniture.

SCREWS –
To loosen Nails and screws which have become rusted into wood may be moved by dropping a small quantity of paraffin oil over them. Allow this to soak it, and after a short time the screws may be taken out. Touching the head of the screw with a red-hot poker, or inserting a screwdriver into the head and tapping it firmly with a hammer will often succeed in starting a stiff screw.

Seagrass matting has a habit of absorbing unpleasant odours. If this occurs, cut up some unskinned onions, put platefuls around the room, close doors and windows, and leave for 48 hours. Then remove the onions and air the room. A few drops of Nilodor at this stage is a good idea.

SEAGRASS MATTING

For sea water stains on fabrics, sponge with warm water to dissolve the salt. If the stain persists, spot with methylated spirits (U.S.A. = Solox), then launder or dry clean. For sea water stains on shoes, try 2 teaspoons of methylated spirits (U.S.A. = Solox) to 1 dessertspoon of milk. Rub on, leave to dry, then repolish.

SEA WATER

Spot with methylated spirits (U.S.A. = Solox), then wash thoroughly.

SEAWEED STAIN

To successfully store seeds, it is important that the seeds reach maturity before picking them from the plant. Spread the seeds to dry either in the sun, or in a warm dry room. When thoroughly dry, dust lightly with a good powder fungicide before storing. Don't store in a container where sweating is liable to occur.

**SEEDS
To store**

See FLOUR.

SELF-RAISING FLOUR

Septic tanks use a natural dissemination of waste with bacteria, so use a good brand of toilet cleaner sparingly. Never use bleach.

SEPTIC TANK

**SHAMPOO –
carpet**

Before shampooing carpet, test a trial patch with the shampoo of your choice. If possible, remove all the furniture from the room then vacuum the carpet. Apply shampoo, clean a small area at a time, and dry as you go so that the carpet remains as dry as possible.

If a mechanical shampooer is being used, do all the room at one time. Leave until the room is completely dry before moving furniture back onto it.

SHEEP SKINS

Some sheep skins particularly those used for invalids or babies, can be readily washed. Usually the washing instructions are marked. If not, rub brown vinegar into the back to stop it from hardening. Then scrub the surface with Woolmix on a rough cloth. Do this in sections so as not to get the skin too damp and as you go, rub each section with a dry cloth.

To cure a sheepskin, first scrape the fat from it and wash with salt and water. Pin the skin out onto a board and pull it tight. Apply a thick paste of soda bicarbonate mixed with lighting blue kerosene. It is most important to use the blue kerosene. Apply this paste every day for 3 days then leave to dry. Scrape and send to dry cleaner.

This method of tanning does not allow for washing the skin at a later date. It must be sent to the cleaners as water washing will harden the skin.

A better method is to buy a Charlton's Tanning Outfit, for a cost of a few dollars and follow the instructions on the pack. The Charlton's method allows the skin to be water washed at a later date.

**SHEEP SKINS
To whiten**

Lay the skin on a flat surface and scour well with warm water and soap. Rinse with clean water and hang to drain. Then hang up to bleach in a large packing case, or some other container which can be made airtight. Put 250 grams (8 oz) of Sulphur in a tin, set it alight and place it under the skin, being careful not to have it close enough to burn the wool. Close all openings, and leave until the next day. Next day, hang out to dry and beat with a broomstick to fluff up the wool.

Out of water, shells always lose their lustre. If they are kept in a jar with water the colour is retained. Coating the shells with vaseline retains the lustre, but the best method is to spread the shells on newspaper and spray with a clear lacquer.

SHELLS

It is best to cover kitchen shelves with wipeable, plastic, self-adhesive material. Wooden shelves which become stained should be washed thoroughly with hot soapy water and wiped down with a solution of one part bleach to 4 parts water. Don't put things back into the shelves until they are perfectly dry.

SHELVES

The surface of trousers and suits can become shiny in parts. Sponge the shiny area with Brown Vinegar, or strong cold tea. Finally, hold the steam iron over the sponged area, but do not press down. Hang in the air to dry.

SHINY FABRIC

SHOE POLISH
To Revive

If shoe polish has gone hard in the tin, add a teaspoon of Mineral Turpentine to the polish and leave it to soak through. Then warm it by placing the tin in a container of boiling water. Make sure the water does not spill into the polish. Stir the turps into the polish and you will have a paste which can be applied to the surface of the shoes once more.

SHOE POLISH
STAIN

Shoe polish on clothes should be dabbed gently with Methylated Spirits (U.S.A. = Solox) on a pad of cotton wool. Hold another pad of cotton wool under the stain to absorb any additional moisture and prevent the stain from spreading.

If shoe polish has rubbed off on to the covering of your chairs, or on the carpet, check if it is coloured or black. Black will need turpentine to remove it, and cleaning fluid is best used for coloured stains. Sponging with almost neat Woolmix also works well.

Don't put wet shoes next to a fire or radiator. Direct heat dries out the leather. Pack the shoes with newspaper which absorbs the moisture, at the same time keeping the shoes in shape.

For dirty shoes or boots, rub over with a clean cloth and cloudy ammonia, then polish.

NEVER STORE BOOTS OR SHOES IN PLASTIC. They sweat and can become mouldy.

TO RESTORE leather shoes or boots, make sure they are clean. Rub with a dry brush to get rid of mud and grit from the seams. Don't forget underneath the heel. Then go over the shoes, both the upper and the sole, with Methylated Spirits (U.S.A. = Solox). Thoroughly dry, then go over the shoes again with Liquid Paraffin, obtainable from chemists or drug stores. Leave for 24 hours, rub with a soft cloth, then polish.

WHITE PATENT LEATHER shoes can be sponged with Methylated Spirits (U.S.A. = Solox) and then sprayed with Preen. Rub off any dirty marks, then finally polish with Tuxan Patent Leather Spray. For crack marks on leather, touch up with a dab of typist's white Correction Fluid.

FABRIC SHOES made from denim or similar material, can be washed or scrubbed with Woolmix.

SCUFF MARKS on shoes can be sponged off with Solyptol on a soft cloth.

SATIN SHOES. Use a good powder carpet cleaner. Just rub the powder into the shoes with the palms of the hands, brush off with a soft cloth.

**SHOES –
To waterproof**

An old-fashioned method of waterproofing shoes and boots is to put 60 grams (2 oz) of Fine white Resin, from hardware shops, 60 grams (2 oz) of Beeswax and 60 grams (2 oz) of Rendered-down Mutton Fat, into a tin with about a litre of Linseed Oil. Stand the tin in boiling water until the beeswax has melted. Apply to the boots or shoes with a cloth or brush.

SHOWER CURTAIN
The hemline of a shower curtain accumulates soap. This can be removed with a paste made of salt and lemon. Rub firmly and then wash in lukewarm water.

SHOWER RECESS
To clean stubborn stains from the shower recess, spray with any good mould stripper, or a fairly strong bleach solution. This will help to clean dull soap residue from the walls and the base of the shower recess. Finally, wipe out the recess with a solution of equal parts of Brown Vinegar and Kerosene.

See also TILES.

SHRUNKEN WOOLLENS
Try dissolving 90 grams (3 oz) Epsom Salts in boiling water. Allow to cool, then soak the garment in the solution for about half-an-hour. After soaking, squeeze out the excess water, stretch the garment to its correct shape, and when almost dry, iron under a damp cloth.

SILICONE
There are no satisfactory solvents for silicone glue which, in liquid form, gets right into the fibres of fabric and sets hard like glass. If you can get at any of the silicones whilst they are still wet, you can remove them. Just mop up, then sponge with eucalyptus. The longer they remain the harder they get. The only way I have found to cope with them is to put a towel over a silicone stain and hammer, so that you crush it as you would glass. That way you may get enough out of the carpet or garment to make it un-noticeable.

When sponging silk, be careful not to leave a water mark. Boil 6 **SILK**
parts of water with 6 parts of alum and sponge the spot while
resting on a towel. Send raw silk to a good dry cleaner. You can
wash pure silk in Woolmix, but hand wash only and rinse.

Or, wash in warm, soapy water with a few drops of methylated
spirits (U.S.A. = Solox) and vinegar. This makes ironing easier.
Iron when almost dry under a clean cloth.

To stiffen silk, put a handful of White Sugar into the rinsing
water, or add a tablespoon of Methylated Spirits (U.S.A. =
Solox).

To keep silk white, add a pinch of Cream of Tartar to the rinsing
water. If already yellow, add a tablespoon of Cream of Tartar,
and let it soak for 10 minutes. A few drops of Methylated Spirits
(U.S.A. = Solox) helps to give silk a sheen.

Before ironing silk garments, put them in a plastic bag in the
freezer for half-an-hour.

To clean silver, put soap powder and boiling water into an **SILVER**
aluminium saucepan and let the silver stand in it for about half-
an-hour. Take out and polish with a dry cloth.

A few drops of Methylated Spirits (U.S.A. = Solox) in the
washing-up water gives an added lustre to silver.

BLACK SPOTS on silver can be treated by rubbing the spots
with a mixture of chalk and kerosene. Leave to dry, then wash in
boiling water.

SILVER CLOTH for polishing can be made by bringing to the
boil, two litres (one quart) of water, two tablespoons of Whiting,
or fine powdered Bon Ami and half-a-cup of household
Ammonia. Put in two clean dusters, stir well into the boiling
solution for at least 10 minutes, then hang on the line to dry. Do
not wring. Store silver cloths in a plastic bag.

TO STORE silverware, sprinkle it with Talcum Powder or Powdered Starch before putting away. Another method is to put a
small lump of camphor in the box in which silver is stored. Or,
keep wrapped in blue tissue paper, Never use rubber bands, as
they tarnish the silver.

SILVERFISH These pests are nearly impossible to eradicate except by professional treatment, but you can deter them by putting Epsom Salts, borax or alum in the back of the cupboards. Some people buy strong smelling soaps to put in the cupboards as a deterrent. Powdered Sulphur, available from chemists, is also good to deter Silverfish.

SIMMER To cook in liquid just below boiling point, which should be continuously, but very gently, bubbling.

SINK A good efficient way to clear a blocked sink, is to put a handful of washing soda, or common salt, down the sink. Then pour in half-a-cup of Vinegar. Leave for about half-an-hour, then pour in boiling water.

Always keep a rubber plunger (from hardware stores or supermarkets) in the cupboard under the sink in case of a blockage.

STAINLESS STEEL sinks will sparkle like new if cleaned with a damp cloth and fine powdered Bon Ami.

Used in soups, sippets are made from stale bread. Dice the bread and saute in hot butter until evenly browned and crisp. **SIPPETS**

Slate is used in many modern homes. To keep it looking fresh, use equal parts of linseed oil and turpentine. This will prevent smudges for quite some time. **SLATE**

If slugs are causing a problem around the house, leave a little beer in the bottom of a can and sink the can where the slugs appear. They drown quite happily. **SLUGS**

Break Rock Ammonia, available from chemists, into small pieces and fill a bottle. Then cover with Lavender Water, Rose Water or Eau do Cologne. **SMELLING SALTS**

See ODOURS. **SMELLS**

Use bleach, one part bleach to four parts water to remove smoke stains. If the smoke stains are on brick, use a scrubbing brush. On paint work, use a cloth and sometimes, a little powdered Bon Ami. **SMOKE STAINS**

SNAILS   An old-fashioned method for ridding the garden of snails is to mix lime, soot and bran together in equal quanitites and sprinkle around the edges of the beds. Lime mixed with salt with also kill snails, but keep the lime away from azaleas.

SNEAKERS   Footwear of this nature is generally made of fabric and should be scrubbed clean with a nailbrush and hot soapy water. Woolmix is good instead of soap as it also freshens. Leave in the sun to dry.

SOAP   Bits and pieces of soap collect in everyone's bathroom. Don't throw them out. Collect the bits and cover with boiling water and a little borax. Boil a few minutes, stir well and cut into blocks when cool.

Another way is to make a small bag of foam plastic, have a drawstring top and fill the bag with the pieces of soap and hang it on the shower or bath tap. This is most economical and children like using it.

HONEY SOAP FROM SCRAPS. Save soap scraps and re-make them into your own personally manufactured soap. Cut left-over soap scraps into small pieces. Soak 1 cup soap scraps and ⅓ cup of a cup of Rolled Oats together with enough water to more than cover them. Simmer the soap and oats mixture with a tablespoon of Honey until it is melted. Stir now and then with a wooden spoon. Add 2 tablespoons of Glycerine to the simmering mixture. Turn the soap mixture out into moulds. This recipe leaves the hands feeling soft and smooth.

SOAP –
To make   To make soap at home, boil steadily for 2 hours, 3 kilos (6 lbs) Clean Fat, 500 grams (1 lb) Caustic Soda, 250 grams (8 oz) Powdered Borax, 250 grams (8 oz) Resin, 10 litres (5 quarts) water. Take off the heat and stir in a cup of Kerosene. To set, pour into a kerosene tin which has been cut lengthwise.

4 cups of plain flour (all purpose), 1 teaspoon bicarbonate soda, 1 teaspoon salt and milk to mix.

METHOD. Mix dry ingredients and add enough milk to make a stiff dough. Cook for one hour in a medium oven.

SODA BREAD

Wine or animal stains on the carpet can often be completely removed by covering with soda water while it is fizzing. Flat soda water is not quite so effective.

SODA WATER

On clothes, sponge off a soft drink stain with a mixture of warm water and Borax. Use one tablespoon of Borax to half-a-litre (1 pint) of water.

SOFT DRINK STAINS

Cover the stain very liberally with salt. Leave for about an hour, then vacuum off. Repeat if necessary.

SOOT STAIN

Spice Ball or Pomander

Spice Balls

Spice balls, or pomanders as they used to be called, can be made with oranges or lemons combined with aromatics — The chosen fruit should be thin skinned without blemishes __

Start at the stalk end, and in circles, press about one cupful of cloves into the fruit until it is covered — On a sheet of tissue paper mix together one dessert spoon of orris root powder (available from chemists) and two dessertspoons of cinnamon — Roll the fruit in the powder, twist the paper around it, and store in a cupboard for a few weeks —

In damp weather it is a good idea to leave the fruit for only two weeks, then put into a very low heat oven to assist the drying process —

The cloves syphon the juice from the fruit which eventually shrinks and hardens — Shake off excess spice powders, tie a ribbon around it, and hang in wardrobe — The spice ball will impart a gentle aroma for about three years —

SPIDERS   Usually seasonal, their trailing webs are great dust collectors. However, they do love a diet of silverfish, so they have their uses. Creosote on a cloth will often discourage spiders.

SPONGE CAKE The trick of making a good sponge cake is to follow a couple of basic rules. The generally accepted recipe has 3 eggs. For a lighter sponge, separate the eggs and beat the whites separately.

RECIPE: Beat 3 egg whites to a peak and gradually add ½ cup Castor Sugar. Beat the egg yolks and fold into the egg whites. Sift 1 cup Self Raising Flour twice, the second time over the egg mixture. Trickle down the side of a mixing bowl 2 tablespoons hot water and fold in. Pour into a well greased tin and bake for 20 minutes at 180 degrees Centigrade (350°F).

SQUID STAIN On the beach you could be unlucky enough to have a squid, or worse its ink over your bathers or towel. As the ink from a squid is a protein stain it should be treated with Borax. Pack the stain with a paste of Borax and water and leave for about 20 minutes. Then let the hot tap run through it. Repeat if necessary. If the garment is white it can then be washed in a weak solution of bleach.

STAINLESS STEEL Methylated Spirits (U.S.A. = Solox) mixed with fine powdered Bon Ami is very good for cleaning stainless steel sinks etc.

STAMPS The keeping of stamps is a fine hobby for young and old. It can be informative and valuable. Removing a stamp from an envelope can be tricky and spoil the serrations. If you put the envelope in the freezer for a few hours, the stamp can be lifted off with stamp tweezers.

To prevent rusting, after use, put steelwool into a jar with a little bicarbonate soda. Leave the lid on and the wool will be rust free.

Another way to preserve steel wool after using it, is to put it into a plastic bag in the freezing compartment of the refrigerator.

STEELWOOL

WHERE DO YOU GET STEEL WOOL?

FROM A HYDRAULIC RAM ...

A piece of wet newspaper over the sticker, and left for 15 to 25 minutes, will usually remove it without much trouble. Another method is to cover the sticker with wet cellophane or plastic. Leave for about half-an-hour. Some stickers remove very easily by smothering them with oil. Another method is to cover them with warm butter or margarine.

**STICKERS
To remove
from glass**

This can be most irritating. To make drawers run more readily, rub the sticking areas with beeswax. A good silicone polish will often do the job just as well.

**STICKING
DRAWERS**

**STRAW
MATTING**

Clean by using a large coarse cloth dipped in salt and water. Wipe the matting dry as you go. The salt will prevent the matting from turning yellow.

Straw or plaited matting will last longer, and keep cleaner, if it is given a coat of clear varnish when new.

SUEDE   If you can get to grease spots quickly with a bottle of soda water, and sponge while the water is still fizzing, the grease spots will disappear. Or sponge with Woolmix and a little warm water. Dry with a hair dryer as you sponge.

Another good cleaning method for suede is to mix together two tablespoons powdered Borax with one tablespoon salt and two teaspoons Dry Cleaning Fluid. Leave on the mark for 24 hours. Rub it in with the palm of your hand. Brush off and repeat if necessary. If suede is shiny, a gentle rub over with very fine emery paper should restore the look of suede.

SUET PUDDING   125 grams (4 oz) flour, pinch salt, 125 grams (4 oz) bread-crumbs, 125 grams (4 oz) chopped suet, 30 grams (1 oz) sugar, 1 teaspoon baking powder and milk to mix.

METHOD. Put the flour, salt, breadcrumbs, suet, sugar and baking powder into a basin, and mix together with the beaten egg and milk to make a soft mixture. Turn into a greased basin and steam for 2½ hours. This is a general recipe, and can be varied by the addition of 30 grams (1 oz) or more of currants, raisins, dates, figs, etc. Butter or margarine can be used instead of suet for a lighter pudding.

No matter how careful we are, the sun still manages to catch the **SUNBURN**
tender skin, particularly of youngsters. The best relief is cold tea.
Saturate a cloth in cold tea and drape over the burnt areas.

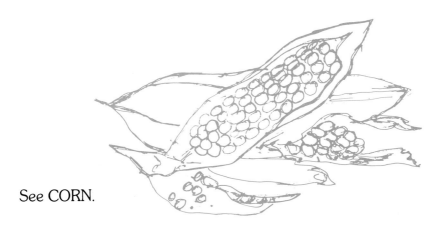

See CORN. **SWEET CORN**

Only use fresh sweetbreads as they quickly spoil. There are two **SWEETBREADS**
sorts, heart sweetbreads and throat sweetbreads. Heart are the
best.

First soak them in lukewarm water for a couple of hours, then
put them into boiling water and simmer gently until firm but not
hard. Now plunge them into cold water and they are ready to be
prepared to the recipe of your choice.

"I suppose that the two questions I'm most often asked about washing woollies are 'How do I stop them shrinking?' and 'What's the best way to dry them?'

The simple answer to both questions is 'with care and gentleness'. Remember, you're not washing a tea towel, you're cleansing a valuable item of clothing. So treat it as such. For a start, use water that's comfortably warm, never hot. And when you hand wash, carefully squeeze the Wool Mix solution through the garment. Those two precautions will help prevent any shrinkage.

Drying woollies presents a problem for all of us in Winter.

However, many of today's pure wool and wool blend garments can stand a gentle spin drying without ill effect. Make sure that you first roll the garment into a sausage shape so that it receives the same pressure all over. You can even tumble dry some woollies but check that the manufacturer says it's safe.

When slow drying, spread woollens flat on two or three thicknesses of bath towels and keep them well away from direct sunlight.

Have you tried Wool Mix for your cashmere and handknits?

They come out wonderfully soft. And in Winter, be sure to use it for such other woollen items as scarves, coats, hats and gloves.

COUNTRY HOMESTEAD
Eucalyptus
WOOL MIX

"I recommend this no-rinse wool mix for a lovely soft wash for woollens"

750ml

HEAT MARKS. Camphorated oil can be rubbed with the grain. **TABLES**
If that is not successful, polish with Brasso.

HOT MILK spilt on a table leaves a nasty white mark which can
be rubbed with a flannel wrung out in hot water and vinegar. For
the next week rub daily with hot Camphorated Oil. If the mark
still remains after this, polish with Brasso, then with good furniture
polish.

See LINEN. **TABLE CLOTHS**

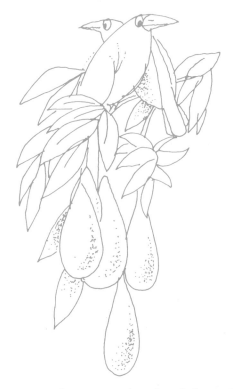

The trees are decorative and grow to a height of about 4 metres **TAMARILLO**
(12 feet). The fruit is most versatile and can be used for jam or
chutney, as well as raw with cold meats, and as a fruit, either raw
or cooked.

The skin of the tamarillo is not pleasant to eat. Skin them by
immersing the fruit in boiling water for a few minutes before
peeling.

165

TAMARILLO JAM 5 kilos (10 lbs) Tamarillos, 2 large Onions, 1 Kilo (2 lbs) Apples, 1 Kilo (2 lbs) Brown Sugar, 1 teaspoon Salt, a little Black Pepper, 1 teaspoon Allspice, ½ teaspoon Cayenne Pepper, 2 litres (1 quart) Brown Vinegar and ½ teaspoon Powdered Cloves. Boil all together for 4 hours, then strain and bottle.

TAMARILLO JELLY Pour boiling water over 1 kilo (2 lbs) Tamarillos and leave for 4 or 5 minutes. Tip off the water and pour cold water over. The skins should now peel off fairly easily. Roughly chop the peeled tamarillos and put into a saucepan with 1 thinly sliced lemon. Add 1 litre (2 pints) of water and boil for half-an-hour. Let the fruit strain through a jellybag overnight. Next day measure the liquid and bring to the boil. Add ¾ of a cup of sugar for every cup of liquid and boil steadily for about 25 minutes. As soon as the jelly will set by testing, remove from the heat and let it stand for a few minutes before pouring into hot, dry jars. Seal when cold.

TAMARILLO SAUCE Use 1½ kilos (3 lbs) of Tamarillos and immerse the fruit in boiling water for a few minutes, so that the skin peels off easily. Drain. Add the juice of 2 lemons and 1 litre (2 pints) of water. Boil the fruit first, then add 1½ kilos (3 lbs) of sugar. If desired, the seeds can be strained out before the sugar is added. Add a small nob of butter to prevent scumming and cook for about ½ an hour, or until it sets by testing a small amount on a saucer.

TAPESTRY

To clean tapestry, make up a mixture of 2 tablespoons Powdered Borax, 2 tablespoons Cooking Salt, 2 teaspoons Dry Cleaning Fluid. Sprinkle that all over the tapestry and rub in with the palms of your hands. Leave for about an hour, then either shake the powder out or beat the tapestry from the back to remove all excess powder.

TAR

On pets paws or carpets, tar can be removed with eucalyptus. Apply the eucalyptus, then sponge with warm, soapy water and repeat half hourly until tar is removed.

TARRAGON

This herb has strongly flavoured leaves and can be used in any meat poultry, fish or vegetable dishes. It will grow from a cutting. The leaves can be blanched and deep frozen.

TATTOO

The sap from the paw paw palm has been used by the natives of New Guinea to fade away tattoos. It needs to be repeated continually until the tattoo marks gradually disappear.

TEAK

To remove the buildup of oil from teak, clean down with a soft cloth and Brown Vinegar. It may be necessary to repeat this two or three times. When oiling teak, use only use teak oil and remember, the oil must always be applied to the cloth first, and never directly onto the wood itself.

TEAPOTS

For SILVER or POTTERY teapots which are stained inside put in 3 or 4 Steradent tablets, half fill the pot with water and leave overnight. For ALUMINIUM, use salt and vinegar on steel wool. ENAMEL teapots can be cleaned on the inside with salt.

To clean the spout, pack with salt and leave overnight. Next morning remove the salt and scald with very hot water.

TEA STAINS
On a TABLECLOTH, tea stains can be removed by packing the stain with Borax, then allowing warm water to run through. Always get rid of the stain before washing. On the CARPET, sponge a tea stain with 1 tablespoon of Borax to ½ litre warm water. Mop dry with a towel so that the carpet does not get too wet.

TEA TOWELS
A good boiling occasionally, in a pan on the stove, with soapy water is a good idea. For teatowels that have become very discoloured, soak them in boiling water with a tablespoon of Borax to every ½ litre of water before boiling.

TEFLON
Never use harsh abrasive on teflon coated cooking utensils. If the Teflon discolours, mix 2 tablespoons of Borax, ¼ cup Bleach and 1 cup water. Boil this solution in the stained pan for 5 minutes. Wash, rinse and dry. Wipe with oil before using.

TERRAZZO
Every now and again terrazzo should be given a good clean with a soft brush, hot water and a weak solution of bleach. When it is thoroughly dry, re-surface with a good beeswax polish.

TERYLENE CURTAINS
These can be very hard to iron if creases are allowed to form during washing. Avoid this by washing the curtains in the bath in almost cold water. Just add detergent and wash the curtains through the water. After rinsing drip dry and rehang before they are quite dry.

TEXTA
Methylated Spirits (U.S.A. = Solox) works for some textas. Nail polish remover can also be effective but as the inks vary so much removing a texta stain is a "trial and error" process.

On CLOTHING, gently dab with essence of lemon. Don't rub as that will spread the colour. On WALLPAPER, try toothpaste to remove texta but use it very gently.

Remember, always check the cure on an inside seam to see how it affects the fabric.

When thawing meat make sure you do so in the refrigerator not outside on the kitchen bench. Frozen vegetables may be thawed by placing the packet in cold water.

THAW

If a thermos smells stale and musty put in a tablespoon of bicarbonate soda, fill with water and leave overnight. Another method is a piece of charcoal kept in the Thermos when it is not in use.

THERMOS

The lid should never be kept on a Thermos when it is not being used.

If a thermos has been used regularly for tea or coffee, it will develop a stain or film on the inside. To clean it, fill the thermos with water, add a couple of Steradent Tablets and leave overnight. Next day give it a good shake with the cap on and rinse out with hot soapy water.

Probably the most versatile of all herbs for cooking. It can be used with meat, in stuffings, tasty sauces, marinades and pate. It gives a wonderful flavour to herb bread and many vegetables.

THYME

Thyme is easy to grow, either in the garden or in pots. For drying, harvest the leafy branches just before they start to flower and make sure you gather them on a dry day before midday. Hang in bunches in a shady, airy place, and when crisp dry, strip off the leaves and seal in airtight containers. The flavour and aroma of thyme is much more penetrating when dried.

The best method for cleaning tiles is to wipe them down with a solution of equal parts Brown Vinegar and Kerosene. For white grouting use a weak solution of bleach and a nailbrush to scrub. For coloured grouting, use Epsom Salts.

TILES

TIMBER STAINS
For timber stains on clothing, sponge with Methylated Spirits (U.S.A. = Solox). If the stain is sap from the timber, try sponging with Eucalyptus.

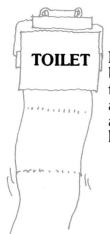

TOILET
Nothing looks worse than a nasty brown rust stain down the back of the toilet. The first thing to do is to have a plumber check the toilet and stop any leaking water. To remove the stain, make a paste of Powdered Whiting, Cream of Tartar, in equal parts, and a few drops of Peroxide. Pack the paste onto the stain and leave as long as possible. Repeat often.

TOMATO Bottled
Use firm, ripe tomatoes. Blanch the fruit in boiling water for 3 minutes, then plunge into cold water and peel. Make a brine, using 1 dessertspoon of salt to 1 cup of water. Pour the hot brine over the fruit. Pack in jars. Fill right to the top with boiling water and seal immediately.

TOMATO CHUTNEY
3 kilos (6 lbs.) tomatoes, 1½ kilos (3 lbs.) onions. Slice and put in separate basins. Cover both with a small handful of salt and leave overnight. Drain both. Put the onions into preserving pan and just cover with brown vinegar. Cook for 10 minutes. Add tomatoes.

Make a paste with 1¼ kilos (2½ lbs.) sugar, 6 tablespoons dry mustard, 4 tablespoons curry powder, 1 teaspon cayenne pepper, and some more brown vinegar. Put this into the preserving pan with the tomatoes and onions, cook for about 1½ hours without the lid.

Firm ripe tomatoes should be used in this recipe. Cover the tomatoes with water and add a teaspoon of Salt, a Bay Leaf and a little Basil. Boil to reduce the liquid. Put the mixture through the mincer and then through a sieve to remove the skin and seeds. Spread on a tray to dry in the sun, or in the oven on a low temperature with the door ajar. Move the pulp round every hour so that it dries evenly. Add oil to moisten. Pour into jars and cover with a little oil to seal.

TOMATO PASTE

To peel tomatoes, plunge them into very hot water for about 2 to 3 minutes. Another method is to hold them over heat on a long toasting fork.

TOMATO Peeling

The best fruit to use when bottling are the firm ripe tomatoes. Blanch the fruit in boiling water for 3 minutes. Plunge into cold water and peel. To make the brine combine 1 dessertspoon of salt to a cup of boiling water. Pour the hot brine over the fruit and pack in jars. Fill the jars with boiling water right to the top. Seal immediately.

TOMATO Preserving

On vinyl, cover the stain with a little methylated spirits (U.S.A. = Solox) on a damp cloth, or sponge with Borax and warm water.

TOMATO STAINS

For soups, stews or casseroles, Tomato Magic is very successful.
To make a sauce with Tomato Magic, mix with water, add salt and pepper, a little vinegar if required. If the sauce is to be used for oysters and other fish dishes, add cream and lemon instead of the vinegar.

TOMATO SUBSTITUTE

TORTOISE SHELL Polish tortoise shell by rubbing with a soft cloth and Olive Oil.

TOWELS To soften towels and make them more absorbent, soak overnight in a solution of water and powdered Borax. Use 1 tablespoon of Borax to 1 litre (2 pints) of water.

TONGUE Tongue is usually soaked in brine by the butcher. The basic cooking for tongue is to put the tongues into a saucepan with 1 large onion, 1 large carrot, 2 or 3 stalks of celery (all the vegetables should be chopped), a few whole peppercorns, cloves, ½ teaspoon of mixed herbs, and several bacon rinds with just enough water to cover.

Bring to the boil, reduce the heat then with the lid on, simmer slowly for 3 hours. Lamb tongues take only about 1½ hours. Remove the tongues, and as soon as they are cool enough to handle, peel and remove the fatty tissue.

If the tongues have not been steeped in brine by the butcher use the same procedure, but include 1½ teaspoons of salt for every sheep's tongues. Tongues can be served with parsley or madiera sauce, or cold with salad.

TREE TOMATO Refer TAMARILLO.

TURKEY Before cooking turkey it is best to know whether it is an old or young bird. An old turkey has rough, reddish legs, a young turkey smooth, black legs. If the turkey is old, it is better to boil the bird, then just finish off in the oven to give a roasted finish.

TYRES Pram tyres should be rubbed occasionally with Glycerine. This not only cleans them, but helps to preserve them.

172

UGG BOOTS

Wash Ugg Boots with Woolmix using about a capful to a bowl of warm water. Rub briskly with a rough towel to dry the surface. Many people put Ugg Boots into the washing machine for cleaning.

UMBRELLA

An old umbrella frame can be used for garden decoration by stripping the cover from it, painting the frame to prevent rust, then plant the opened umbrella into a large pot of soil or in the garden. Grow ivy or a flowering creeper beside it and trail the runners up over the frame. This makes a very spectacular display.

Another use for an old umbrella is to turn it into a useful clothes-dryer. Remove the fabric, paint the frame with a good enamel paint to stop it from rusting, and suspend it by the handle. For those confined to a flat, it can be used over the bath, or is excellent for drying garments where direct sunlight should be avoided, by hanging under a verandah or a tree. You will be amazed at the extra hanging space your old umbrella will provide. When not in use it can be folded and stored away.

UNDERLAY

Carefully choose an underlay which will not stain too badly if something is spilt on the carpet. Remember, anything you spill on the carpet will possibly go through to the underlay and you don't want a stain from the underlay coming up to the surface of the carpet.

UNGLAZED QUARRY TILES

Improve the look of unglazed quarry tiles by mopping over with a mixture of half Linseed Oil and half Turpentine. It's a good idea to wash the tiles first with hot soapy water and a little Cloudy Ammonia and allow it to be thoroughly dry before applying the linseed oil mixture.

UPHOLSTERY

Stains on upholstery should be moved according to the fabric specification. For suede or velvet, do not use a water cleaner. Only a powder cleaner is suitable for this type of fabric. Never spot or clean upholstery without first testing the fabric in a part that will not show if it marks.

URINE STAINS

On a mattress, this stain is sometimes very difficult to remove as it soaks through to the padding. Try covering the stain thickly with a mixture of Borax and Imperial Leather talcum powder. Then cover the whole area with a towel, and for preference, leave 2-3 days. Remove the powder then sponge the surface with cloudy ammonia or white vinegar.

A new mattress cover can be purchased and slipped over the existing one if the stain is too bad to remove.

On DRAPES, sponge quickly with a cloth and cloudy ammonia. If stain remains, drapes should be cleaned by professional cleaners.

Make sure your vacuum cleaner is regularly emptied. Pick up any hairpins or other objects which are lying about the carpet as they could damage the motor. Regular servicing is a good idea if the vacuum cleaner is to last a lifetime.

VACUUM CLEANER

See THERMOS

VACUUM FLASK

Precious and sentimental possessions can have more value than you imagine. Make sure you have them valued regularly and it is a good idea to have either photographs or sketches of everything which is of any value. This makes life much easier in case of burglary, both for regaining possession of valuables, or for claiming the insurance.

VALUABLES

To clean varnish, rub with equal parts of raw Linseed Oil and Kerosene. Mineral Turps is sometimes helpful.

VARNISH

On carpet, use kerosene to get rid of a vaseline stain, but dab, don't rub.

VASELINE

CRYSTAL vases, particularly those which are difficult to get to the bottom of, can be washed with warm soapy water with a little cloudy ammonia and a few broken eggshells. Shake vigorously and rinse thoroughly with warm water.
POTTERY vases should be sealed on the inside with beeswax before using them. Just melt the wax and coat the inside of the vase using a small brush.

VASES

Roast veal can be dry, and should always be cooked in an oven bag. Before placing it in the bag, cover the piece of meat with oil and a little plain flour (all purpose) mixed with dry mustard. salt and pepper. A few bacon rinds add flavour to the meat. When the meat is cooked, split the oven bag and use the juices to make gravy.

VEAL

VEGETABLES
To keep

Green topped vegetables such as carrots, beetroots and turnips keep better if the tops are removed before storing. Store them in a brown paper bag, never use plastic. The paper absorbs some of the moisture and the plastic can make them sweat and quickly deteriorate.

Leafy vegetables such as lettuce and cabbage, again should never be stored in plastic. Wrap them in kitchen paper and keep in a vegetable drawer of the refrigerator.

VEGETABLE
STAINS

Most vegetable stains can be removed with borax and warm water, using 2 tablespoons of borax to 1 litre (2 pints) of water.

VEILS

Before packing away, make sure a wedding veil is clean. Pack in plenty of pale blue tissue paper in a cardboard box with some Epsom Salts sprinkled in the bottom of the box but not touching the veil.

If a veil needs stiffening use gum water. Another method is to iron the veil with greaseproof paper.

Also see WEDDING VEIL.

Crushed, or rain-spotted velvet should be steamed. This can be done by hanging in the bathroom and leaving all windows and doors shut when taking a shower or filling the bath. Another method is to hold a steam iron over the back of the velvet. Under no circumstances should you press down with the iron onto velvet as it will flatten the pile.

VELVET

FURNITURE covered with velvet can be freshened by lightly rubbing with a chamois leather wrung out in hot water with a few drops of Cloudy Ammonia in it. For cleaning, use a good powder cleaner.

MILK STAINS on velvet can be treated by making a fairly thick paste with Cream of Tartar and cold water. Pack the paste over the stain, leave it to dry, then vacuum off. Any residue from the stain can be treated with a good powder carpet cleaner. Rub it it gently with the palm of your hand, leave it overnight then brush off.

FLUFF ON CORDED VLEVET. Hang the garment in the bathroom to steam, then brush off with a dry cloth or a chamois leather dipped in warm water and wrung out.

Venison is a very dry meat and if possible should be cooked in an oven bag. Another method is to lightly dust a joint of venison with flour, pepper and salt, then put onto the rack of a baking dish with pieces of bacon over the top of it. Put it into a hot oven for 15 minutes, reduce the temperature, and pour 1 cup of boiling water into the pan. Cook until tender, allowing 15 minutes to every 500 grams (1 lb.) and baste every 15 minutes. Serve with red currant jelly.

VENISON

VERTICAL GRILL　This is a most satisfactory and quick way of cooking as the fat runs into the tray at the bottom. In order to stop the smoking, put a crust of bread in the tray, or add a cupful of water. Stand the grill on a few layers of newspaper to prevent the fat from splattering.

VINYL　Vinyl floors sometimes develop a buildup of polish, particularly around the edges. This can be treated with Kerosene on steel wool, then washed with very hot water and detergent. In heavy traffic areas where there are scuff and scratch marks, try rubbing with a little Brasso or a paste of powdered Bon Ami and Methylated Spirits (U.S.A. = Solox).

FURNITURE AND CAR UPHOLSTERY of vinyl, need a certain amount of care to prevent cracking. Wash regularly with any good detergent, and polish with Saddle Soap or a Cream Polish.

VOMIT　Vomit on clothing can usually be removed by sponging or washing in a solution of water and borax. Another method is to wash the garment in Woolmix as this will remove any odour. If there is a lingering smell of vomit in the bathroom or in a car, put a few drops of Nilodor to a pad of cotton-wool and leave around the area.

WALLPAPER

Washable wallpaper is easily cleaned with warm water and a little cloudy ammonia. Non-washable wallpaper poses a problem particularly with grease stains. Make a paste of talcum powder with very little water and allow to dry on the stain, then brush off with a soft cloth.

Bread will also clean wallpaper. It must be 2 days old. Remove all the dust from the wallpaper first, then hold the bread in the hand and wipe lightly over, changing the bread as its surface becomes dirty. Vinyl wallpaper can be cleaned with white vinegar on a warm cloth.

**WALLS —
To clean**

Painted walls are a good project for the spring cleaner. During the winter months, heating, condensation and dust gather on the walls, giving them a rather tired look. A bucket of hot soapy water and about 8 tablespoons of Powdered Borax with a cup of Cloudy Ammonia will do wonders to brighten walls.

**WALNUT
FURNITURE**

If the furniture is genuine walnut, a scratch or stain can be removed by cutting a whole walnut and rubbing the mark vigorously with the nut. The juice will remove the stain. Water marks on walnut furniture can usually be removed with Brasso.

WALNUTS

TO KEEP. Leave the walnuts in the shell and put them into an earthenware pot. Fill the pot almost to the top then cover about 2 inches thick with sawdust. Place the pot in a cool dry place.

TO PICKLE Walnuts, put them in a saucepan of brine and gently simmer for about ½ hour. Pour off the brine then spread the walnuts flat to finish draining. Leave them in a nice dry place until they become black, then make a pickle of vinegar, adding to every litre, black pepper, and 30 grams (1 oz.) each of ginger, shallots, salt and mustard seeds.

WARTS Break a thistle off and put the milk that runs from the stem onto the wart. This usually makes them disappear very quickly.

Another cure for warts is equal parts of kerosene, lemon juice and castor oil. This mixture shuld be applied three times a day for a week.

WASHING MACHINE To keep a washing machine clear of lint and soap build-up, put a packet of Epsom Salts in the detergent container and run the machine through a clear cycle. Do this regularly and the washing machine will remain clean.

WASPS Wasps, unlike bees, can sting a number of times. If the sting is left in one of the wounds, it must be removed. A strong solution of baking soda helps to relieve the pain.

WASHING DISHES If you are machine washing dishes make sure that the detergent you use is suitable not only for machine but for the dishes that you wash. Do not wash good china which has gold leaf on it in a dishwashing machine.

WASHING GLASSES If glasses look smeary after washing, or if beer goes flat in them, you must change your washing method. Use hot water and Morning Fresh detergent. When the glasses have been thoroughly washed make sure they are well rinsed with hot water and drain only. Do not use a tea towel.

Water, particularly in some country areas, tends to leave a sediment build-up in kettles. A glass marble in the bottom of the kettle will prevent this from happening.

If water is hard, add a little Borax to the washing up water and also for washing clothes.

ON LEATHER, water stains are most difficult to remove. Whether it is a shoe or a handbag, try wiping it over with a soft cloth and a little Brown Vinegar. This will sometimes remove the water mark.

ON FABRIC. If colours are light, a weak solution can sometimes help. A hot cloth wrung out in a solution of Cloudy Ammonia can also be helpful.

ON FURNITURE, water marks can sometimes be removed by rubbing the area with a little cigarette ash mixed with water. Be sure to rub with the grain of the wood. If you are a household of non-smokers, try a little Camphorated Oil, or Brasso.

WATER

These make a wonderful exotic-looking table decoration. To keep them looking their best and always fully open, drop a little melted wax in the centre of the flower.

WATERLILIES

Shoes and boots should be waterproofed before wearing them. Use Tuxan Silicone Water Repellent. Clothes which are waterproofed should be cleaned only by a commercial cleaner with the facility to reproof the garment after it has been cleaned.

To make your own waterproofing mixture for boots and shoes, see SHOES.

WATER-PROOFING

WATER BEDS If the mattress is made of vinyl, it is not sufficient to just change the sheets. The underlay must be aired regularly because perspiration can build up and encourage the growth of mould. The water inside the mattress must contain a fungicide. Some manufacturers recommend using a fungicide additive every three to four months.

When buying a water bed make sure you get one which is on casters. This makes it easy to move about. With any new purchase, read the instructions carefully and follow them.

WAX Applied to curtain rods, wax will help curtains to slip on easily.

Wedding Anniversaries

First Year	— Paper	Thirteenth	— Lace
Second	— Cotton	Fourteenth	— Ivory
Third	— Leather	Fifteenth	— Crystal
Fourth	— Books	Twentieth	— China
Fifth	— Wood or Clocks	Twenty-fifth	— Silver
		Thirtieth	— Pearl
Sixth	— Iron	Thirty-fifth	— Coral
Seventh	— Copper Bronze or Brass		Jade
		Fortieth	— Ruby
		Forty-fifth	— Sapphire
Eight	— Electrical Appliances	Fiftieth	— Gold
		Fifty Fiftieth	— Emerald
Ninth	— Pottery	Sixtieth	— Diamond
Tenth	— Tin or Aluminium		
Eleventh	— Steel		
Twelfth	— Silk or Linen		

TO STORE. First have the wedding gown cleaned by a professional cleaner. Do not store a wedding gown in plastic. Pack it in pale blue tissue paper. Take it out and hang it in the air every two or three months if possible. A sprinkling of Epsom Salts with the wedding gown, but not touching it, will help to keep any moths away. **WEDDING DRESS**

TO KEEP a wedding cake, wrap in two layers of brown paper, then store in a cardboard box in a cool dry place. Add some Silica Gel, (available from cake decorators) to the container, but be sure the Silica Gel does not touch the cake. Another method is to put into a freezer bag, pump all the air out, and store in the freezer. **WEDDING CAKE**

TO STORE a wedding veil, do not fold, but roll in blue tissue paper. Every few months it should be taken out and re-rolled in the opposite way. Store away from light. **WEDDING VEIL**

TO MEND wedding veils, the old-fashioned method was to darn over small tears with hair. Another method is to dip a small piece of veiling into raw thin starch, place it over the tear, then cover with a handkerchief and press on the wrong side with a warm iron when the starch is dry.

Also see VEILS

Weevils can get into any jar or packet and ruin good food. Do what our country grandmothers did. Tape a few bayleaves to the lid of the container and the weevils will disappear. For dried fruit, add a twist of lemon rind into the jar. **WEEVILS**

WEIGHT

TO PUT ON. Make up 5 tablespoons of sugar, 2 tablespoons powdered skim milk, 1 tablespoon Aktavite, 1 egg and 1 litre of milk. This quantity will probably last a couple of days.

WINDOW CLEANER

Use equal parts of kerosene, cloudy ammonia, methylated spirits (U.S.A. = Solox), and water. If kerosene does not mix well, a good shake before using is sufficient. This mixture is particularly good for seaside areas. After washing windows with the mixture, polish with a soft dry cloth.

Another good window cleaner is to mix together 4 dessert-spoons Cornflour with half-a-cup Cloudy Ammonia and half-a-cup brown Vinegar. Shake well to mix the cornflour through and apply to the window using a slightly dampened sponge. Rub over with scrunched up newspaper.

WILD DUCK

After having plucked and wiped the bird, leave it in milk for at least an hour, then stuff it with forcemeat. Do not overspice. Roll in flour and brown in butter. Put in a moderate oven and bake with the milk in which the bird was soaked. When nearly done, lift out the bird and make gravy. Brown equal parts of flour and butter and break down with the liquid in which the bird has been cooking.

Strain the gravy, then add a glass of port wine and a dessert-spoon of red currant jelly. Pour over the bird in the casserole and cook slowly until quite tender.

185

WINE STAINS   Fresh wine spilled on clothing or carpet should be treated immediately with soda water. Pour the soda water onto the stain, mop up, working from the outside to the middle so as not to spread the stain. Repeat if necessary.

If the stain has been left to dry, moisten the area, then pack with Borax and leave to dry before vacuuming off. Repeat if necessary.

WINE IN COOKING

Wine softens the connective tissue of meat and improves the texture of cheaper cuts.

Wine give an extra tang to simple stews and casseroles, soups, or sauces.

Wine in food loses its alcoholic content. The heat evaporates the alcohol.

As a general rule, white meats are best cooked with white wine, and red meats with red wine. Lamb, veal and game fall into either category.

WINE TRIFLE   Cut cake into slices or cubes. Arrange in the serving dish and dot with jam. Moisten with sherry, and if the cake is stale, a little ginger ale is a good idea. Make a custard and pour over the cake. Let it cool, and decorate with fruit, chopped jelly or coconut.

WOK

With increased popularity in Chinese cooking, the wok has become an additional utensil in many kitchens.

New woks often have a type of plastic film over the inside surface which must be removed before the utensil is used. Fill the wok with water, add a tablespoon of bicarbonate soda and let it come to the boil, then rub with a firm brush. When the surface is completely clear, dry it, smear all over with oil, then heat the wok to temper it.

WOOD

HEAT MARKS on highly polished wood can usually be removed with Brasso.

CIGARETTE BURNS are best treated with toothpaste.

CANDLEGREASE. Put ice in a plastic bag and sit it over the candlegrease for a few minutes. Scrape off as much as possible, rub the area with a few drops of eucalyptus on a soft cloth, then polish.

SCRATCHES. If you can't remove scratches, try hiding them. For dark wood, iodine or Kiwi dark tan shoe polish is good. On light wood, a shoe polish to match the colour, and if you can't get an exact match, use a lighter shade and keep repeating to build the colour up.

WOODWORM or BORER can be treated with kerosene. Be sure to get the kerosene into all the little holes. When you're certain that all the little crawlies, and their eggs, are destroyed, fill the holes with wood filler and polish.

See also WALNUT, CEDAR AND MAHOGANY.

See SALAD BOWLS.

WOODEN UTENSILS

WOOLMIX RECIPE

Martha Gardener has been sharing this recipe with her radio audience for 30 years. It is an old fashioned recipe, which has survived many generations.

4 cups soap flakes, 1 cup methylated spirits, 50 mls. eucalyptus. In U.S.A., substitute methylated spirits with Solox or Rubbing Alcohol.

This home-made mixture is thick, like mashed potato, and you use about 2 tablespoons to a bowl of warm water and DO NOT RINSE.

The commercial product, manufactured by Kiwi, has been made to pour from a bottle and like the home-made mixture, there is no need to rinse.

To straighten wool before reknitting, roll it around the ironing board, cover with a damp cloth, and iron. Another way is to roll into balls and put into the pressure cooker for two minutes, or microwave for 30 seconds.

WOOL

Winter woollens, knitted or woven, often develop little balls of fluff. A piece of dry foam rubber or foam plastic, rubbed over the garment, will usually take it off, or use a tea towel wrung out in warm water.

WOOLLENS
Pilling

Wash woollens before storing, Silverfish are attracted to un-washed garments. A few cakes of unwrapped Imperial Leather, or some other highly scented soap, in among the woollens also assists in keeping moths and silverfish away. It is a good idea to take the garments out to air about once every two months.

Powdered sulphur deters silverfish.

WOOLLENS
Storing

If a jumper has been stretched, try washing it by hand in luke warm water and Woolmix. Wrap it in a towel to get out as much water as possible. Then lie it flat to dry, pushing it back into shape on a dry towel. If the jumper is too stretched for treatment to work, it would be better to undo it and start again. Another method is to simply undo the bands and knit onto them to make them tighter.

WOOLLENS
Stretched

Woollen garments which have shrunk can sometimes be res-tored by dissolving 90 grams (3 ozs.) Epsom Salts in boiling water. Allow it to cool, then soak the garment in the solution for about half-an-hour. Squeeze out excess water, lie the garment flat, stretch it to its correct shape and size, and when almost dry, iron it with a damp cloth over the top of the garment.

WOOLLENS
Unshrinking

WOOLLENS
To wash

With the use of Woolmix, washing woollens is not a problem. The no rinse method saves a lot of effort and works better than conventional washing. Heavy garments, which take longer to dry, can be rolled in a towel after washing, then put in the washing machine to spin dry on slow cycle. Do not put woollens in the sun to dry. Direct sunlight can discolour the wool.

WOOLLENS
To whiten

Soak overnight in warm water and a little Napisan. Wash the next day and dry away from direct sunlight. It is better for woollens to dry as quickly as possible.

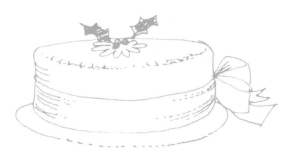

250 grams (½ lb.) butter, 500 grams (1 lb.) sugar, 9 eggs, 500 grams (1 lb.) plain (all purpose) flour, 125 grams (4 ozs.) self raising flour, 500 grams (1 lb.) currants, 500 grams (1 lb.) sultanas, 500 grams (1 lb.) raisins, 250 grams (½ lb.) dates, 125 grams (4 ozs.) almonds, 60 grams (2 ozs.) cherries, 185 grams (5 ozs.) mixed peel, 1 teaspoon essence of lemon, 1 teaspoon essence of almond, ½ teaspoon nutmeg, 1 teaspoon ground ginger, 1 teaspoon cinnamon, ¼ teaspoon powdered cloves, ½ cup brandy, sherry or rum.

XMAS CAKE

METHOD: Prepare fruit, blanch and slit almonds, chop peel, put into a bowl and add spirits. Cover and leave for at least two hours. Now line the cake tin with one layer of brown paper. Foil or greaseproof paper can be used instead of the brown paper.

Cream the butter and sugar, then add eggs one at a time and beat well as each egg is added. Add the peel and essence. Sift in the flour and spice, mixing well. Two-thirds fill the cake tin, making a shallow hollow in the centre of the cake. Bake in a slow oven for 5 to 6 hours. Leave in the tin until the cake is cold.

This mixture can be divided and cooked in two tins, in which case it will take 3 to 4 hours to cook.

XMAS MINCE

250 grams (8 ozs) each of raisins, sultanas, currants, and apples, 125 grams (4 ozs) chopped peel, the rind and juice of 1 lemon, 1 cup brown sugar, 1 tablespoon golden syrup, 1 teaspoon each of nutmeg, allspice and cinnamon, ½ teaspoon salt, 30 grams (1 oz) butter, 3 tablespoons rum or brandy.

METHOD. Peel and grate the apples and put them into a basin with the dry ingredients. Add the lemon and syrup. Melt the butter with the spirits and thoroughly mix with all the ingredients. Store in screw top jars in a cool dark place, or in the refrigerator.

XMAS PUDDING CLOTH

To successfully remove the cloth from the Xmas Pudding, the preparation is most important. Prepare the cloth before mixing the Xmas pudding, First plunge it into boiling water to sterilise it, then wring out and spread on a flat surface and liberally sprinkle with flour. This method causes the flour to adhere to the cloth rather than to the pudding, so that it can be removed without taking any of the surface of the pudding with it.

Here are three different ways to make your own yeast:

YEAST
Home made

1.   Save about 1½ litres of potato water. When cold add 1 tablespoon flour, 1 tablespoon sugar, pour into jug or preserving jar, adding 1 teaspoon compressed yeast (or old yeast). Make during morning, and by evening it should have a frothy top, ready to use. After taking some out each time, leave enough in the jar to start the next lot. Replenish with cool potato water and above quantities of flour and sugar each day. Do not add any more compressed yeast.

2.   30 grams hops, 1 cup flour, 2 tablespoons sugar, 2 litres water. Boil hops for a few minutes in a small quantity of water. Drain and add sufficient to make 2 litres. Add sugar, and when tepid also flour. Just shake it in and never mind it if it seems lumpy. Grate in medium sized raw potato. Bottle. If you have a little yeast in the bottle to start working, it can be used the same night. With home made yeast it takes longer for the bread to rise than compressed yeast. Divide it into 3 bottles, leaving sufficient room to work. Each bottle makes about 1½ kilos of flour.

3.   Six breakfast cups of cold water, ½ handful of hops, 2 medium potatoes. Cut but do not peel the potatoes. Add the water and hops, and boil about half an hour. Have ready 2 tablespoons of flour, mixed with 1 tablespoon of sugar. Strain again through a fine sieve. Bottle when nearly cold, and put in a light warm place.

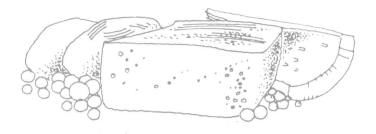

YORKSHIRE PUDDING 125 grams (4 ozs.) plain (all purpose) flour, ¼ teaspoon salt, 2 eggs, 1 cup milk, ¼ cup water.

METHOD: Sift the flour and salt into a bowl and make a well in the centre. Drop in the eggs and mix with a wooden spoon, adding about half the milk and water a little at a time, and drawing in the flour to make a thick smooth batter. When all the flour has been drawn in, beat the batter very well until air bubbles rise to the surface and burst. Then stir in the rest of the liquid and leave the batter to stand in a cold place for at least 1 hour. This gives the starch grains time to swell and burst and produces a lighter pudding. Melt about 30 grams (1 oz.) dripping in a meat tin and when it is smoking hot pour in the batter and bake for about 3 minutes in a hot oven.

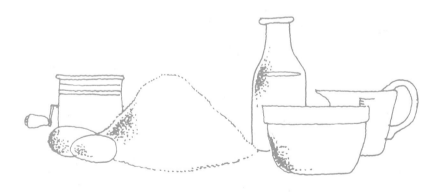

If a zip fastener becomes stuck, talcum powder liberally sprinkled over the teeth often helps to free it. Lead pencil is also effective but take care it doesn't mark your clothes. Zippers sometimes stick because of fabric from the inside hem holding back into the zip. Try to jiggle it loose rather than cut it. **ZIPPER**

ZUCCHINI BREAD

3 eggs, 2¼ cups castor sugar, 3 teaspoons vanilla, 1 cup oil, 2 cups grated zucchini, 3 cups plain (all purpose) flour, ¼ teaspoon baking powder, 1 teaspoon salt, 1 teaspoon bicarbonate soda, 3 teaspoons cinnamon, 1 cup chopped walnuts.

METHOD. Beat eggs until light and fluffy, add sugar, vanilla and oil. Beat until thick. Stir in grated zucchini. Sift flour and baking powder, salt, soda and cinnamon. Fold into zucchini mixture with chopped walnuts. Pour into two greased loaf tins and bake in a moderate oven for 1¼ hours.